Nikola Müller

Mining Omics Data

Nikola Müller

Mining Omics Data

From Correlation to Independence

Südwestdeutscher Verlag für Hochschulschriften

Impressum / Imprint

Bibliografische Information der Deutschen Nationalbibliothek: Die Deutsche Nationalbibliothek verzeichnet diese Publikation in der Deutschen Nationalbibliografie; detaillierte bibliografische Daten sind im Internet über http://dnb.d-nb.de abrufbar.
Alle in diesem Buch genannten Marken und Produktnamen unterliegen warenzeichen-, marken- oder patentrechtlichem Schutz bzw. sind Warenzeichen oder eingetragene Warenzeichen der jeweiligen Inhaber. Die Wiedergabe von Marken, Produktnamen, Gebrauchsnamen, Handelsnamen, Warenbezeichnungen u.s.w. in diesem Werk berechtigt auch ohne besondere Kennzeichnung nicht zu der Annahme, dass solche Namen im Sinne der Warenzeichen- und Markenschutzgesetzgebung als frei zu betrachten wären und daher von jedermann benutzt werden dürften.

Bibliographic information published by the Deutsche Nationalbibliothek: The Deutsche Nationalbibliothek lists this publication in the Deutsche Nationalbibliografie; detailed bibliographic data are available in the Internet at http://dnb.d-nb.de.
Any brand names and product names mentioned in this book are subject to trademark, brand or patent protection and are trademarks or registered trademarks of their respective holders. The use of brand names, product names, common names, trade names, product descriptions etc. even without a particular marking in this works is in no way to be construed to mean that such names may be regarded as unrestricted in respect of trademark and brand protection legislation and could thus be used by anyone.

Coverbild / Cover image: www.ingimage.com

Verlag / Publisher:
Südwestdeutscher Verlag für Hochschulschriften
ist ein Imprint der / is a trademark of
AV Akademikerverlag GmbH & Co. KG
Heinrich-Böcking-Str. 6-8, 66121 Saarbrücken, Deutschland / Germany
Email: info@svh-verlag.de

Herstellung: siehe letzte Seite /
Printed at: see last page
ISBN: 978-3-8381-3505-2

Zugl. / Approved by: München, LMU, Dissertation, 2012

Copyright © 2013 AV Akademikerverlag GmbH & Co. KG
Alle Rechte vorbehalten. / All rights reserved. Saarbrücken 2013

Abstract

Biological studies across all omics fields generate vast amounts of data. To understand these complex data, biologically motivated data mining techniques are indispensable. Evaluation of the high-throughput measurements usually relies on the identification of underlying signals as well as shared or outstanding characteristics. Therein, methods have been developed to recover source signals of present datasets, reveal objects which are more similar to each other than to other objects as well as to detect observations which are in contrast to the background dataset. Biological problems got individually addressed by using solutions from computational sciences according to their needs. The study of protein-protein interactions "interactome" focuses on the identification of clusters, the subgraphs of graphs: A parameter-free graph clustering algorithm was developed which was based on the concept of graph compression, in order to find sets of highly interlinked proteins sharing similar characteristics. The study of lipids "lipidome" calls for co-regulation analyses: To reveal those lipids similarly responding to biological factors, partial correlations were generated with differential Gaussian Graphical Models while accounting for solely disease-specific correlations. The study on single cell level "cytomics" aims to understand cellular systems often with the help of microscopical techniques: A novel noise robust source separation technique allowed to reliably extract independent components from microscopic images describing protein behaviors. The study of peptides "peptidomics" often requires the detection outstanding observations: By assessing regularities in the data set, an outlier detection algorithm was implemented based on compression efficacy of independent components of the dataset. All developed algorithms had to fulfill most diverse constraints in each omics field, but were met with methods derived from standard correlation and dependency analyses.

Contents

1	**Introduction**	**1**
1.1	Motivation	1
1.2	Synopsis	5
1.2.1	Interactome Clustering with PaCCo	5
1.2.2	Partial Lipidome Correlations with dGGM	8
1.2.3	Membrane Proteome Dependencies	11
1.2.4	Cytome Source Separation	13
1.2.5	Outlier Detection in Peptidome with CoCo	15
1.3	Outline	18
2	**Background**	**19**
2.1	Dataset Formalities	19
2.1.1	Matrices	19
2.1.2	Graphs	20
2.1.3	Random Variables	20
2.2	Correlation-based Networks	21
2.3	Data Transformations	22
2.3.1	Singular Value Decomposition	22
2.3.2	Principal Component Analysis	24
2.3.3	Independent Component Analysis	24
2.4	Dimension Reduction	26
2.5	Data Compression	27

2.5.1	Data Communication		27
2.5.2	Coding Costs		29
2.5.3	Entropy		31
2.6	Data Mining		32
2.6.1	K-means Clustering		33
2.6.2	Evaluation Measures		33
2.7	Related Algorithms		36
2.7.1	Data Transformation		36
2.7.2	Graph Clustering		38
2.7.3	Outlier Detection		40
3	**Shared Features in Weighted Graphs**		**43**
3.1	Biological Question and Data		44
3.1.1	Interactomes		44
3.1.2	Interactome Clustering		45
3.1.3	The Yeast Synthetic Lethal Interactome		46
3.2	Weighted Graph Clustering with Simulated Annealing		48
3.2.1	Simulated Annealing Algorithm		48
3.2.2	Performance on Interactome		51
3.3	Improved Weighted Graph Clustering with PaCCo		52
3.3.1	Motivation		53
3.3.2	Designing Novel PaCCo Algorithm		55
3.3.3	PaCCo Algorithm Design		58
3.3.4	PaCCo Cluster Representatives		58
3.3.5	k-PaCCo Bisecting Strategy		63
3.3.6	PaCCo Splitting Strategy		64
3.3.7	Benchmark Results of PaCCo		67
3.4	Conclusion and Outlook		79
4	**Differential Dependencies**		**81**
4.1	Biological Question and Data		82

4.1.1	Lipidomes	82
4.1.2	Lipidome Correlations	83
4.1.3	The Human Glioblastoma Lipidome	83
4.2	Conventional Correlation Networks	87
4.2.1	Gaussian Graphical Model	88
4.2.2	Regularized Gaussian Graphical Models	90
4.2.3	Lipidome GGM Results	91
4.3	Differential Gaussian Graphical Model	93
4.3.1	Motivation	93
4.3.2	dGGM Design Principle	95
4.3.3	dGGM Algorithm	96
4.3.4	dGGM of the Glioblastoma Lipidome	99
4.4	Conclusion and Outlook	106

5 Image Pattern Dependencies — 107

5.1	Biological Question and Data	108
5.1.1	Membrane Proteome	108
5.1.2	Membrane Proteome Analyses Today	108
5.1.3	The Yeast Plasma Membrane Proteome	109
5.2	Quantification of Spatial Patterning	112
5.2.1	Qualitative Observations	112
5.2.2	Image Quantification by Network Factor	113
5.3	Sole Pairwise Dependence	116
5.3.1	Quantification Coefficients	116
5.3.2	Linearization of Manders Coefficient	117
5.3.3	Numerous PM Protein Domains	119
5.4	Non-Random Dependence Measure	121
5.4.1	Minor Dependence on Intensities	121
5.4.2	Major Dependence on Domain Pattern	123
5.5	Conclusion and Outlook	130

6	**Independent Source Separation**		**131**
6.1	Biological Question and Data		132
6.1.1	Cytomes		132
6.1.2	Cytome Source Recovery		132
6.1.3	Yeast Cdc42 Cytome Establishing Polarization		133
6.2	Manual FRAP Curve Fitting		135
6.2.1	Source Recovery of FRAP with SAM-SOBI		136
6.2.2	Benchmarking FRAP Analyses With SAM-SOBI		136
6.3	Conclusion and Outlook		142
7	**Outstanding Feature Detection**		**143**
7.1	Biological Question and Data		144
7.1.1	Peptidome		144
7.1.2	Peptidome Real Dataset Description		144
7.2	Supervised Outlier Filtering		145
7.3	Unsupervised Outlier Detection with CoCo		147
7.3.1	Introduction		147
7.3.2	CoCo Bottom-Up Outlier Detection		149
7.3.3	Regularity Estimates with CoCo		150
7.3.4	Outlier Classification by Coding Costs		157
7.3.5	CoCo Benchmark Results		159
7.4	Conclusion and Outlook		166
8	**Conclusion**		**167**
8.1	Summary		167
8.2	Future Directions		172
A	**References**		**175**
B	**Abbreviations**		**193**
C	**Index**		**195**

D Glossary

1 Introduction

1.1 Motivation

Life science experiments produce vast amounts of data virtually on a daily basis. Especially the recent technological advances in experimental setups produce constantly increasing amounts of heterogeneous and complex high-throughput data across every molecular complexity level. Biologists are overwhelmed by these enormous data amounts, since the essential and desired information is no longer easily accessible by manual analyses. To cope with high-throughput data, knowledge discovery in databases (KDD) offers a large variety of extensive data analysis and mining techniques. KDD approaches comprise not only statistical methods but also machine learning algorithms. The analysis of novel datasets is equally challenging and requires the development of novel and intelligent KDD solutions.

In order to discover the knowledge hidden in datasets, two opposing approaches exist in computer sciences: Supervised information retrieval learns knowledge from the dataset with expert knowledge. Unsupervised approaches require no *a priori* knowledge and use only the intrinsic data information for retrieval. Either approach uses information on object similarities or dissimilarities across any kind of data type. For example, in numerical datasets, objects are characterized by a vector determining the objects location in a multi-dimensional space. The object similarities may then be determined through metric functions of the data space. In network datasets, objects are nodes in a graph connected by edges. Node similarities may then be defined by the concept of strong linkage between nodes. In general, knowledge on object relationships is required to finally reveal the desired information from complex datasets.

To define the information retrieved from datasets, individual life science fields are considered separately. The individual life science fields covered in my doctoral dissertation are put together in the context of biological objects types. The suffix "*-omes*" is typically used for each type of object analyzed in the respective field. For example, the set of all proteins present in one organism is called it's *proteome*. When referring to the studies conducted to analyze an *-ome* the suffix "*-omics*" is used. Figure 1.1 depicts only those *-omes* covered in my doctoral dissertation and how each field is biologically linked. Single cells (*cytomes*) comprise all classes of biological molecules, like proteins (*proteome*) which are themselves assembled by peptides (*peptidome*). Cells are encompassed and also compartmentalized by membranes, which are in turn mostly built of proteins (*membrane proteome*) and lipids (*lipidome*). The cell's ability to live is furthermore based on the principle of interacting molecules (*interactome*) allowing cells to respond to its environment as well as to any external and internal signals. Each field faces new problems when analyzing their respective datasets as a result of their technological advances in experimental setups.

All "*-omics*" studies have their own experimental methods screening for each biological object, the *-omes*, in order to answer individual research questions. Each *-omics* produces datasets of various types. We further characterize each dataset type covered by the mentioned *-omes*.

Numeric Datasets. *Peptidomics* and *lipidomics* analyze the set of all peptides and lipids present in cells, respectively. Their analysis methods yield lists of peptide and lipid measurements generated by e.g. mass spectrometry (MS). MS instruments are originally used to solely identify each molecule. For example, identified peptides provide the information on the present proteins. To avoid inferring false protein information, the false peptide identifications have to be compu-

1.1 Motivation

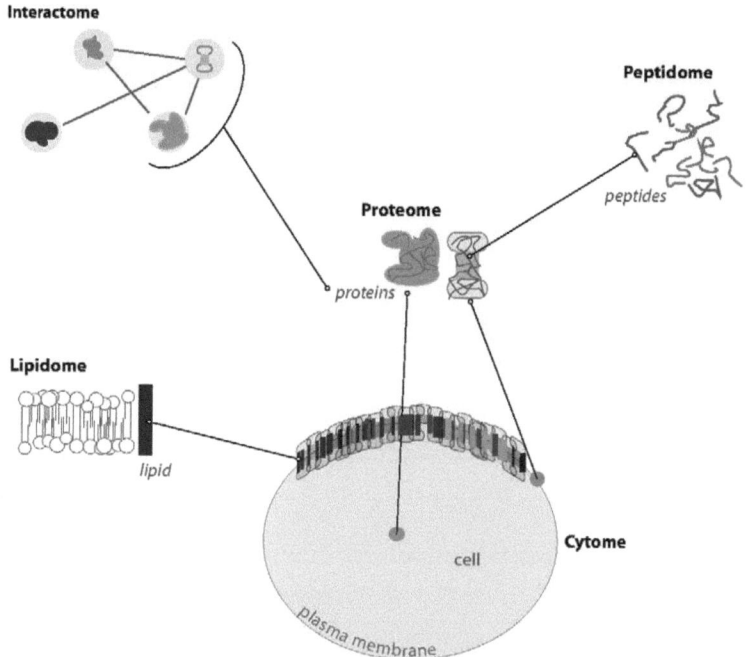

Figure 1.1: Different "-Omics" Sciences and Their Research Objects. Studies on various biological objects for individual research areas, the *-omics*. Sets of single cells is called *cytome*, while their studies is called *cytomics*. Each cell is encompassed by the plasma membrane (PM) and compartmentalized by various membranes (not depicted here). The PM contains proteins and lipids, while the set of all lipids in a cell is its *lipidome*. The membrane proteins together with the remaining pool of proteins in a cell is a cell's *proteome*. Each protein is assembled by single peptides (*peptidome*) while their pairwise interactions is combine in a protein-protein interaction (PPI) network – one type of *interactome*. Depicted are only *-omes* covered by my doctoral dissertation.

tationally detected. Today, MS is sensitive enough to yield absolute abundance information in addition to the list of identified molecules. For example, when comparing disease and control measurements the computation of abundance differences helps to find affected mechanisms.

Image Datasets. *Cytomics* comprises analyses on single cells usually using (fluorescent) microscopy thereby generating a large amount of images showing protein localizations in space over time. Automatic image analysis facilitates handling of complex image datasets and helps to extract the desired features required to draw conclusions on a protein's behavior. Constant technical improvements of microscopes offer new optical perspectives while simultaneously challenging automatic image analysis methods. For example, a new microscope technique enables to visualize the *proteome* subset on the plasma membrane (PM). Protein patterning and colocalization captured in resulting images allow to infer lateral protein behavior.

Graph Datasets. *Interactomics* captures studies of existing molecular interactions on e.g. protein level. Systematically the entire *proteome* is screened for pairwise interactions, while today the strength of interaction is also measured. Resulting PPI networks were typically clustered for strong interlinkage. The additional information on interaction strength is a novel challenge for finding strongly interlinked protein groups.

The research on my doctoral dissertation focused on solving new biological problems with suitable KDD techniques. Therein, methods were developed likewise covering the retrieval of shared or dependent as well as independent or outstanding features of molecular objects. Biological problems were solved by designing new techniques to fit the respective biological research questions.

1.2 Synopsis

The following sections briefly glance at the five novel methods developed during the research on my doctoral dissertation. All developed methods fulfilled most diverse constraints in each -*omics* field, but were met with methods derived from standard correlation and dependency analyses. Each method helped to answer a different biological question.

1.2.1 Interactome Clustering with PaCCo

The question in *interactomics* focused on the identification of clusters in graphs: We developed a parameter-free graph clustering algorithm based on the concept of graph compression (Figure 1.2). By compressing a graph as good as possible, the communication costs between a sender and receiver are minimized. As a result we found sets of highly interlinked proteins sharing similar characteristics.

The identification of protein groups in a PPI network (*interactome*) is a computational challenge. Subgroup identification was accomplished via

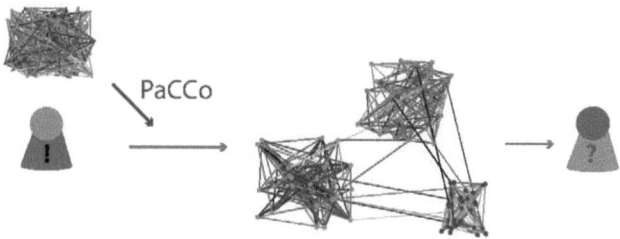

Figure 1.2: Weighted Graph Clustering with PaCCo. Graph information should be transferred from a sender (!) to a receiver(?) with minimal communication costs. To reduce communication costs we compress the entire graph by exploiting graph linkage and edge weight information. Best compression then corresponds to strong graph clustering.

graph clustering, which finds groups based on node interaction profiles. Earlier research was mainly focused on clustering of unweighted graphs while the weighted graph clustering algorithms were not able to converge in a reasonable time. Moreover, present algorithms failed to produce meaningful clustering results for an *interactome* dataset with an unusual edge distribution. This dataset resulted from a high-throughput, organism-wide screen of genetic interactions in yeast.

In Chapter 3, a novel weighted graph clustering method will be introduced outperforming other methods in effectivity, runtime and biological relevance. Then novel algorithm *PaCCo* was designed to solve the following three problems:

Problem 1. Graph clustering is computationally complex, however, *PaCCo* should not suffer from high runtime, thus be efficient. More precisely, the clustering runtime should not (exponentially) scale with graph size.

Problem 2. Algorithm parameter setting require prior knowledge on the dataset structure, which is not known for novel real world datasets. *PaCCo* should not rely on any parameter settings. The user should not have to specify e.g. the number of clusters.

Problem 3. Since real-world graph datasets were generally noisy due to experimental limitations, *PaCCo* should be robust to noise.

To solve all three problems in one algorithm, clustering was brought together with the principle of data compression. The fundamental idea was that a good graph cluster structure was exploited to efficiently compress the entire graph when trying to transfer its details. Strong compression allowed to reduce the data communication costs, thus, reflected the best clustering structure for a graph. To numerically evaluate compression costs the Minimum Description Length (MDL) principle was applied.

1.2 Synopsis

For the first time, data compression was exploited for weighted graph clustering. We developed a fully automatic algorithm, which was not only noise robust but also clustered parameter-independently in a reasonable time. The problems were solved as follows:

Solution 1. Although global optimization techniques provided the most optimal results for a given problem, their heuristics usually suffer from high runtimes while scaling drastically with the dataset size. Thus, *PaCCo* employed an efficient k-means strategy to partition a graph into node sets with respect to interaction profiles. The iteration between cluster assignments and learning of cluster properties was demonstrated to be very efficient, even for large graphs.

Solution 2. By exploiting the principle of data compression, *PaCCo* was parameter-free. A bisecting strategy was coupled to the k-means approach. Independent of the parameter "*k*" the number of clusters were obtained during runtime. After each bisection step, data compression of the subgraph with and without its bisection was calculated to decide whether further splitting was necessary.

Solution 3. Noise resistance was not explicitly formulated. However, the integration of the MDL principle was already sufficient to better cope with considerably more noise edges than other weighted graph clustering algorithms. By using coding costs, the algorithm intrinsically avoids too fine-grained clustering structures (imagine noise to be clustered into single-node clusters), since single-node clusters were generally more expensive than coding each node without additional cluster information. As a result, MDL balanced between opening not too many single-node clusters and without starkly interfering with the overall cluster structure.

In addition to the problems solved, *PaCCo* featured simultaneous clustering of two information types in weighted graphs: One, the node connectivity of a cluster was maximized inside one cluster and minimized to the remaining nodes; Two, the edge weights of one cluster were maximized for similarity. During clustering, the weight distribution of all edges in a cluster was learned from the cluster members. Since *PaCCo* was based on compression principles, the information types determining a cluster were easily decoupled from the clustering strategy. As a result, information types might be adjusted or replaced to fit other needs.

PaCCo was demonstrated to be an efficient and robust weighted graph clustering algorithm which was also parameter free. Benchmark results on synthetic datasets showed that *PaCCo* outperformed other weighted graph clustering algorithms with respect to efficiency, parameter-independence and robustness.

Finally, *PaCCo* was applied to a genetic interaction network from an organism-wide synthetic lethality screen in yeast. We analyzed clustering strength with graph modularity and evaluated whether clusters contained functionally enriched proteins. *PaCCo* was able to outperform other weighted graph clustering algorithms not only with respect to clustering strength but also generate biologically relevant clusters.

1.2.2 Partial Lipidome Correlations with dGGM

The *lipidomics* dataset of disease and control lipid abundance profiles called for disease-specific correlation analyses (Figure 1.3): To reveal those lipids similarly responding to biological factors, we generated partial correlations while accounting for solely disease-specific correlations.

Generating correlation-based networks from *lipidome* profiles allows to reveal lipid co-response patterns. The resulting networks promote understanding of underlying regulatory pathways and help answering given biological or medical problems. Studies, which solve these problems, usually conduct experiments with many control samples and only one or few sample(s) of interest (SOI). For correlation-based analyses, the experimental

1.2 Synopsis

study design has to be taken into consideration. Especially false positive correlations may occur when correlations were calculated from the entire dataset whereof solely few data points were actually biologically relevant.

In Chapter 4, the new principle of a differential Gaussian Graphical Model (*dGGM*) will be introduced. We addressed the drawback of conventional partial correlation analysis when the biological relevance of individual samples was important.

Problem Conventional partial correlation analysis used the entire dataset including all samples to calculate a Gaussian Graphical Model (GGM). The contribution of each sample was never considered, although many biological problems call for a differential consideration. Experiments were often designed in a way that few samples were actually of interest while remaining samples were considered experimental controls. With this background information, partial correlations should ideally only emerge, when the SOI played an outstanding role. In other words, if a partial correlation is already significant on the control samples, the partial correlation should not be included in the results.

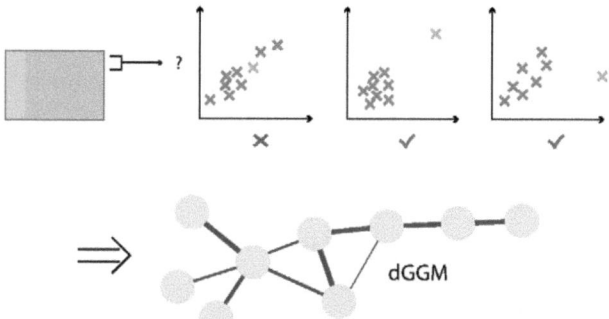

Figure 1.3: Disease-specific Correlations with dGGM. From abundance measurements, pairwise partial correlations are evaluated whether they are related the the disease samples (orange) or control samples (green). This differential analysis of individual partial correlations yield a *dGGM* graph of solely disease-specific correlations.

To overcome the drawback of conventional GGM analysis, a *dGGM* was developed which took the contribution of the SOI into account. The idea of a *dGGM* was to dissect each sample's contribution to a correlation by always leaving one sample out for individual GGM calculations. This approach was inspired by jackknife resampling and revealed all biologically relevant correlations.

The *dGGM* method was solving the problem of SOI-relevance as follows. For simplicity, a correlation relevant to the SOI (here also called "disease-sample") is further referred to as "disease-specific" correlation. The concepts of disease-specificity and disease-unspecificity were used to design the principle to assemble a *dGGM*.

Solution To unravel the disease-specificity of a correlation, each correlation was classified by the way the SOI contributed to the correlation significance. Subsequently, only correlations classified as disease-specific were assembled in the *dGGM* whereas disease-unspecific correlations were rejected. We distinguished significant from insignificant correlations when calculating individual GGMs on the entire or on a truncated dataset. From all significant correlations of the entire dataset, a correlation was classified as unspecific if it originated alone from the control samples. In other words, unspecific correlations were always significant irrelevant of the sample left out – even when leaving out the SOI. In contrast to disease-unspecificity, disease-specificity combined two scenarios. On one hand, a correlation was significant on the entire dataset while the correlation lost significance when excluding just the SOI. On the other hand, a correlation was never significant whenever the SOI was part of the calculations, but gained significance once the SOI was excluded: these correlations followed the idea of a suppressed correlation.

Whenever few samples are responsible for the experimental readout, a *dGGM* is the approach of choice since results were not only filtered for true positives but also completed by the suppressed – but disease-specificity – correlations.

The *dGGM* was developed for and applied to a *lipidome* dataset of an effective perturbation of the Glioblastoma. Lipid levels of an immortal cell line of a Glioblastoma primary brain tumor were quantified. Their pairwise response patterns were analyzed for specificity to the effective perturbation with gene therapy prior to chemotherapy. Results demonstrated that the list of relevant correlations was drastically reduced compared to conventional GGMs while providing novel insights to subsequent Glioblastoma *lipidome* changes.

1.2.3 Membrane Proteome Dependencies

Systematic studies of *membrane proteomics* aimed to reveal organizing principles: We developed automatically and unbiased methods, for extracting protein behavior of one- and two-color images (Figure 1.4). Results of extensive dependency analyses were compared to random expectations. Our developed methods allowed to find responsible factors driving lateral organization of membrane proteins.

Today's knowledge on lateral protein distributions within the plane of the PM is entirely based on non-systematic studies. To advance understanding of the *membrane proteome* a comprehensive and systematic microscopy study was conducted in yeast. Experimental results yielded a new and large image dataset visualizing single as well as pairwise protein distributions.

Problem 1. For quantifying or characterizing single distributions, no analysis methods exist today.

Problem 2. For pairwise distribution analyses no method was universally established.

The sole application of the few present techniques to the new image dataset was not sufficient to better understand protein domain formation. Novel methods were to be designed in order to pinpoint biological factors driving lateral protein distributions in the PM.

In Chapter 5, extensive methods to analyze single and pairwise protein distributions were developed.

Solution 1. Cells in single fluorescent images were first resolved into histogram features. Normalized cumulative histograms were then converted to a numeric factor quantifying the characteristics of a protein distribution pattern.

Solution 2. The overlap of pairwise protein domains was initially quantified with an intensity-based coefficient. The coefficient alone did, however, not allow to draw any conclusions from the co-formation of domains. For improved interpretation of the overlap coefficients, protein colocalizations were correlated to random expectations. Therein, intensities of protein patterns per cell were shuffled within each color channel. In addition, protein patterns were maintained while

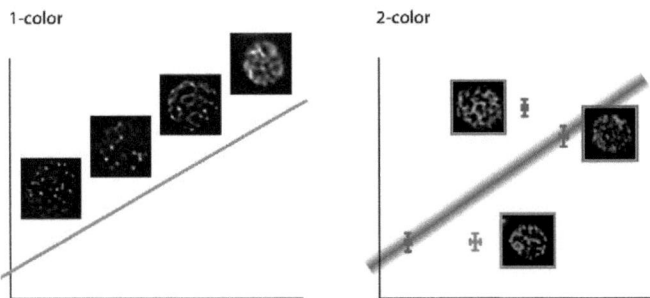

Figure 1.4: Dependencies of Membrane Proteome. Automatic analysis of one-color images allowed to calculate a continuous spectrum of protein patterns. The analysis of two-color images showed that protein patterns influenced membrane protein colocalization (gray values and example image of two proteins with gray border). Few proteins colocalized better (magenta) or worse (cyan) than to be expected.

1.2 Synopsis

the channels of independent cell images were randomized to generate decoy cells.

With the developed methods we showed that many protein domains coexist in the PM forming a more complex view of the PM than previously assumed. Domain coexistence was demonstrated to be random but dependent on the domain pattern formed. The extensive analysis of a new *membrane proteome* dataset allowed to better understand the mixing behavior of proteins in the yeast PM.

1.2.4 Cytome Source Separation

In *cytomics*, the aim was to understand cellular systems with the help of microscopical techniques (Figure 1.5): A novel, noise-robust source separation technique allowed to reliably extract independent components from images describing protein behaviors.

To extract values of protein mobilities on single cell level is a challenging task in high-resolution microscopy. Observable were only the fluorophore distributions of a protein while a protein's mobility may be inferred by selectively photobleaching the proteins and recording their subsequent behavior

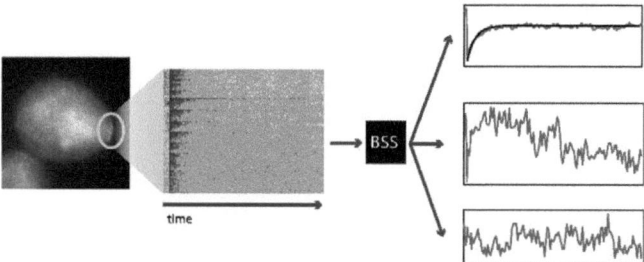

Figure 1.5: Independencies of Cytome. Images of specialized microscopy experiments were sent to a BSS method. Experiments resolved protein distributions over time. Automatically independent component analysis succeeded in separating by protein behaviors from unspecific noise sources.

over time. Usually whether and how fast fluorescence intensities recover over time is collected in a single time-series curve.

Problem 1. Fluorescence intensities of the microscopy images underlie noise fluctuations generated by the microscope setup and maybe the fluorophores. Algorithms not robust to noise will infer false protein mobility information.

Problem 2. The typical stepwise procedure to compute the time-series curve from intensity values acquired from the Fluorescence Recovery After Photobleaching (FRAP) time-lapse movies relied on careful analysis avoiding several pitfalls.

Foremost, the stepwise procedure only accounted for noise fluctuations in the signals through data averaging while more sophisticated methods existed which allowed to explicitly extract noise from mixed distributions.

In Chapter 6, a noise-robust Blind Source Separation (BSS) technique will be applied to yeast *cytome* data. More specifically, an Independent Component Analysis (ICA) variant, called SAM-SOBI, accounted for noise fluctuations without affecting the source separation. The application of SAM-SOBI to the FRAP experiments showed two advantages:

Solution 1. SAM-SOBI was robust to noise present in the *cytome* data. Actual underlying source signal were detected while noise was transferred to separate independent components. Never were source signals mixed with noise in the components.

Solution 2. When applied to the FRAP experiments, SAM-SOBI was able to replace the stepwise procedure. Protein dynamics were accurately reproduced in a noise reduced manner. Time scales of the protein dynamics were best maintained by SAM-SOBI.

The application of SAM-SOBI was demonstrated to be superior to the typical stepwise procedure and also to other ICA algorithms. Thus, source separation techniques in *cytome* data provided a powerful tool to reveal protein mobilities.

1.2.5 Outlier Detection in Peptidome with CoCo

For a *peptidomics* dataset, we developed an algorithm to detect outstanding observations: By assessing regularities in the dataset (Figure 1.6), we based the outlier detection algorithm on compression efficacy.

To detect peptides with unusual features within a *peptidome* is crucial for high-throughput protein identification via peptides. Irregularities in the *peptidome* may distort the deduced protein information. Algorithms detecting only those peptides which deviate disproportionally from the other – regular – ones were strongly parameter-dependent and assumed a fixed data density for the entire dataset. Moreover, underlying data distributions were not always known prior to data analysis. Outliers may be falsely detected or overlooked, especially if the distribution or density assumption was not captured correctly.

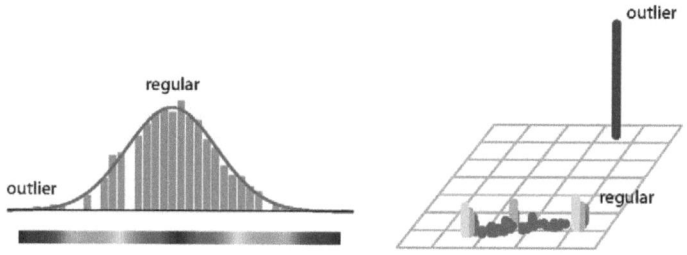

Figure 1.6: Detection of Outstanding Features. We evaluated for each object whether it was part of or outlying the regular dataset. Since regular data were better compressed than outliers, the coding costs of outliers were higher. Consequently, outliers were easily detectable.

In Chapter 7, a novel parameter-free outlier detection algorithm will be introduced. The design of the effective, unsupervised outlier detection method *CoCo* addressed the general problems of outlier detection.

Problem 1. Outliers were generally only spotted in a dataset when the remaining objects were considered normal or "regular". Subsequently, outliers are only identified without any doubt, if the cluster structure of the regular data is known. This cluster-to-outlier dependence equally affected clustering and outlier detection methods: On one hand, clustering quality was affected by its ability to handle or remove outliers; On the other hand, outlier detection effectivity was impaired by misjudging the underlying cluster structure.

Problem 2. Defining "outlierness" always necessitated to also specify the concept of the underlying cluster structure. Likewise important to clustering as well as outlier detection, object density and distribution were never assumed to be equal throughout the data space. For example, clusters with higher and lower density may coexist in one dataset. Therein, objects of low density clusters were easily falsely classified as outliers while true outliers in close proximity to the high density cluster were overlooked. Since any information on the density or distribution of the objects in the data space was unknown especially for real-world datasets a fully automatic method should account for unequal density distributions.

Problem 3. Simple approaches classified outliers when a given density threshold was exceeded – or even simpler solely selected a fixed number of outliers. These thresholds were used as input parameters although the exact value was not always reliably set. In contrast, users rather consult outlier detection methods in order to find all true outliers instead of predefining their number or a density threshold. If a fixed

1.2 Synopsis

characteristic of the outliers was already exactly known before, the outliers are easily detectable.

To solve all three problems and combine their solutions in one approach, the novel outlier detection method *CoCo* coupled a flexible definition of regular data to data compression. The idea was to define a reliable measure of outlierness. To that end, coding costs of each object in the dataset were determined with respect to a variable vicinity which was automatically selected during runtime. *CoCo* solved the problems of outlier detection as follows:

Solution 1. *CoCo* evaluated each object by first placing it into clusters and then deciding whether it was considered an outlier or not. Measured by coding costs, objects were explicitly evaluated for outlierness with respect to an optimal cluster. In principle, with increasing neighborhood size, each object was screened for fitting into potential clusters: If a good compression is achieved, the object is safely classified as a regular object. Whenever best possible coding costs were comparably high, the object was classified as outlier. The coding costs were again numerically determined with the MDL principle.

Solution 2. The underlying cluster substructures in the dataset are arbitrary. Thus, *CoCo* implemented a method detecting not only differently shaped but also potentially distorted clusters. First, ICA removed possible rotation and distortion effects. Second, the equalized data distribution was estimated by the Exponential Power Distribution (EPD), a third-order statistics. The combination of ICA with EPD allowed *CoCo* to identify cluster structures in a flexible manner.

Solution 3. Coding costs of outliers in the dataset substantially differed from the costs of regular data points. The discrepancy of outlier and regular objects was exploited by simply partitioning the objects' coding costs. As a result, *CoCo* did not require any parameter settings.

Notably, the range of the coding costs indirectly adjusted itself to data shape, size and density of each dataset.

The entirely unsupervised algorithm *CoCo* learned the underlying data distribution during runtime in order to detect the number of outliers in a numeric dataset without knowing how many to select.

By exploiting the MDL principle to detect outliers in a fully automated and parameter-free manner, *CoCo* outperformed other outlier detection methods. With respect to usability, major drawbacks were overcome: The number of outliers to be identified were found automatically and no density parameter had to be specified. On synthetic data, *CoCo* was able to identify precisely all outliers in a dataset which included not only an arbitrary number of outliers, but also clusters with variable density and shape.

Finally, *CoCo* was applied to *peptidome* measurements. When compared to a supervised filtering procedure, *CoCo* performed equally well without relying on any *a priori* information.

1.3 Outline

The individual five research projects on my doctoral dissertation are described in detail in Chapters 3–7. Chapters are generally ordered by the object characteristics to be extracted from the complex datasets: form objects sharing similar features, through statistical dependencies and independencies to object with outstanding features. Background information required for more than one chapter is provided in Chapter 2. Finally, Chapters 8 sums up all scientific contributions made during my doctoral work and gives potential future directions.

2 Background

2.1 Dataset Formalities

Let o be an object in the database DB with size $n = |DB|$. Let f be the features in the corresponding feature space F with size $m = |F|$. Each individual feature f characterizing o is either numeric or categoric. Features are also called variables and objects are also called samples.

2.1.1 Matrices

In the matrix-notation of a dataset, the matrix A holds values a_{ij} of objects o_i specified by features f_j as

$$A = (a_{ij})$$

with dimensionality $n \times m$. The matrix rank $\text{rank}(A) = r$ is the maximal number of linearly independent rows or columns. For example, the rank of the identity matrix I_n is $\text{rank}(I_n) = n$.

Any $n \times n$ matrix A is invertible, also called regular, if a matrix A^{-1} exists with $MM^{-1} = I_n = M^{-1}M$. M^{-1} is the inverse of M. Only matrices with $\text{rank}(A) = n$ are invertible.

The eigenvectors v and eigenvalues λ of a square matrix A exist if $Av = \lambda v$. Figuratively speaking, v will be stretched by the factor λ when being multiplied by A without changing directionality of v.

2.1.2 Graphs

Object-to-object relationships are formalized in a graph $G = (V, E)$. G contains a set of $V = (v_i, \ldots, v_n)$ vertices and a set of E edges. The vertices, or nodes, are nothing else but the database objects $v \in DB$. An edge $e_{ij} \in E$ indicates a connection between nodes v_i and v_j. G is also stored in an adjacency matrix A containing $n \times n$ entries of the form

$$a_{i,j} = \begin{cases} w_{ij} & \text{, if } e_{ij} \in E \\ 0 & \text{, otherwise} \end{cases}$$

with w_{ij} being the numerical weight of edge e_{ij}. If the graph is undirected, the matrix is symmetric. If the graph is unweighted, the weights are all equal $w_{ij} = 1$.

2.1.3 Random Variables

Consider a DB with objects o characterized by a set of numerical variables $X = \{X_1, \ldots, X_n\}$. Consequently, any variable X_i is composed of all $(1 \ldots n)$ object values $o \in DB$ as $X_i = (x_{1i}, \ldots, x_{ni})$.

The first-order statistics of X_i is the variable's (arithmetic) mean

$$\mu(X_i) = \frac{\sum_{i=1}^{n} x_{ij}}{n}.$$

The variance (var) and standard deviation (σ) of one variable X_i are

$$\text{var}(X_i) = \sigma^2(X_i) = \frac{1}{n} \sum_{j=1}^{n} (x_{ij} - \mu)^2$$

for a finite population size n. To measure the joint change of two random variables X_i, X_j, the covariance is defined as

$$\mathrm{cov}(X_i, X_j) = \sum_{k=1}^{n} \frac{(x_{ik} - \mu_{X_i})(x_{jk} - \mu_{X_j})}{n}$$

with $\mu_{X_i} = \mu(X_i)$ and $n \neq \infty$. Variance is subsequently a special case of the covariance with $\mathrm{var}(X_i) = \mathrm{cov}(X_i, X_i)$. For the entire set of all variables in X, the $n \times n$ covariance matrix $\Sigma = (\sigma_{ij})$ holds all pairwise covariances $\sigma_{ij} = \mathrm{cov}(X_i, X_j)$.

2.2 Correlation-based Networks

The standard measure of correlation between two variables (X_i, X_j) is the Pearson product-moment correlation coefficient $\rho_{ij} = \rho(X_i, X_j)$, which quantifies *linear dependency* as

$$\rho_{ij} = \frac{\mathrm{cov}(X_i, X_j)}{\sigma_{X_i} \sigma_{X_j}}.$$

For all variables of a dataset, all pairwise correlations are collected in a (Pearson) correlation matrix $P = (\rho_{ij})$. Consequently, the correlation matrix P may also be composed of the covariance matrix Σ via $\sigma_{ij} = \rho_{ij}\sigma_i\sigma_j$.

Another correlation measurement is partial correlation coefficient, which determines conditional dependency. Indirect correlations are diminished resulting in a partial correlation matrix Z calculated by

$$\Omega = (\omega_{ij}) = P^{-1}$$

and

$$Z = (\zeta_{ij}) = -\omega_{ij}/\sqrt{\omega_{ii}\omega_{jj}}.$$

From correlation-based matrices, correlation-based networks G – weighted and (un)directed graphs – are constructed. Vertices are the variables linked by their correlation coefficients. Only the statistically significant correlation coefficients are included in the graph G.

Traditionally, a correlation network is generated from ρ_{ij} while a GGM is generated from ζ_{ij}.

2.3 Data Transformations

Real-world data is usually a mixture of signals. The original signals are not known but contribute to the observed or measured data. In addition, their mixing remains elusive when raw data was not yet transformed. The raw dataset is a $n \times m$ matrix $X = (x_{ij})$ across n samples and m variables.

The transformation of the dataset is accomplished with BSS. BSS searches for the original sources underlying the data and separates them without any knowledge on their mixing or sources. When searching for the sources, they are assumed to be uncorrelated. More specifically, when recovering the sources several source properties may be recovered from the data. For example, sources are assumed to be mutually orthonormal (orthogonal with unit length), statistically uncorrelated or statistically independent whereby the methods to yield sources with these three properties are Singular Value Decomposition (SVD), Principle Component Analysis (PCA) or ICA.

2.3.1 Singular Value Decomposition

SVD for the $n \times m$ matrix A (and $m \geq n$) the SVD is defined as

$$X = UDV^T.$$

with $I_n = U^T U = V^T V$ (Berry et al. 1995, Wall et al. 2003). The columns of U form an orthonormal basis for the variables with $\dim(U) = m \times n$,

2.3 Data Transformations

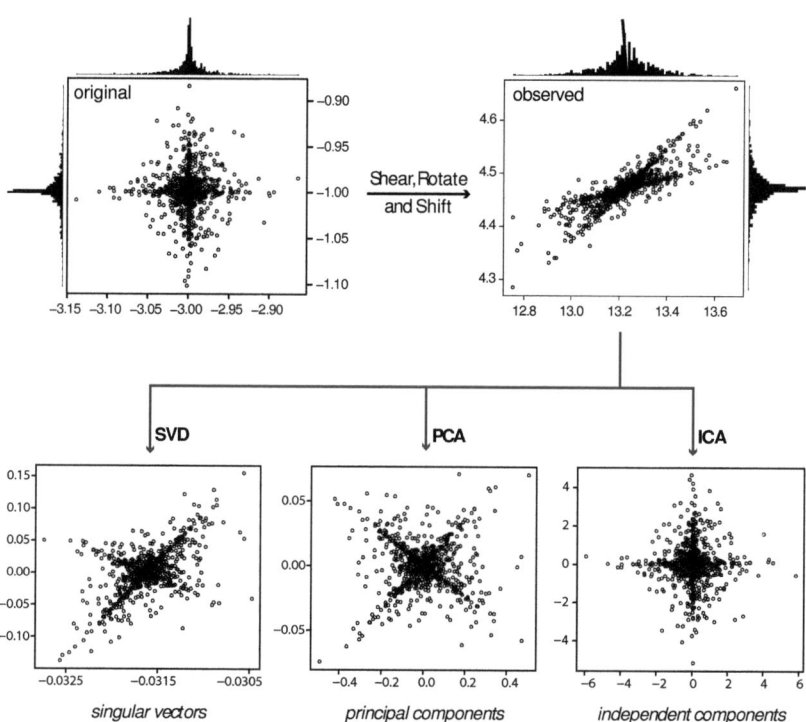

Figure 2.1: Data Transformation with BSS. The original data matrix in the 2-dimensional space was normally distributed in each dimension (x and y). To mimic an observed dataset, the original matrix was sheared, rotated and shifted. On the observed matrix three BSS variants were applied: SVD and PCA yielded singular vectors and principal components of original data estimates, respectively. Both algorithms did not restore the original dataset. ICA yielded independent components, which recovered the underlying original data.

while rows of V^T form an orthonormal basis for the samples with $\dim(D) = \dim(V^T) = n \times n$. The matrix D has only nonzero entries on the diagonal as

$$D = \mathrm{diag}(d_1, \ldots, d_n)$$

Given the rank$(A) = r$, eigenvalues are $d_i > 0$ for $1 \le i \le r$, whereas $d_j = 0$ for $j \ge r + 1$. The *singular values* are then defined as the diagonal elements d_i of D which are nothing else than the nonnegative square roots of the n eigenvalues of AA^T. The singular values are recovered in U (Figure 2.1).

2.3.2 Principal Component Analysis

PCA searches for a linear transformation to maximize variance in the dataset X. As a result the principal components (PCs) of X are orthogonal (Figure 2.1). In contrast to SVD, PCA centers the data before decomposing the covariance matrix of X instead of X.

First, X gets centered around its empirical mean in each dimension by $X_c = X - (\mu_{X_1}, \ldots, \mu_{X_n})$. The mean subtraction assures that the first PCs are those of maximal variance, otherwise the first PC would correspond to the mean. Second, the centered data X_c needs to be normalized to unit variance in all directions to X_c^1. Finally, PC are determined by eigen decomposition of the covariance matrix $\Sigma(X_c^1)$ with

$$\Sigma(X_c^1) = V \Lambda V^T$$

where V and Λ are orthogonal matrices containing the eigenvectors and eigenvalues of $\Sigma(X_c^1)$, respectively.

2.3.3 Independent Component Analysis

ICA searches for a linear transformation to minimize entropy in the dataset X. Compared to PCA, the independent components (ICs) can also be non-

2.3 Data Transformations

orthonormal (Figure 2.1). Thus, a mixing matrix is calculated to describe the shear of the IC basis.

The ICA problem (Comon 1994) is to derive a set of statistically ICs in s^*, which multiplied with a matrix M result in X

$$X = Ms^* + v$$

while considering an additional noise component v. Since the noise underlies an unknown distribution, the recovery of exactly s^* is generally impossible. As a result, the problem definition of ICA is simplified to

$$X = As$$

where A is a mixing matrix to transform the components in s.

To solve the ICA problem, the resulting components s have to be maximized for statistical independence

$$s = WX$$

with a linear transformation of X and a weight matrix $W = A^{-1}$ (A^{-1} is the pseudoinverse of W). The overall projection of the original data into ICs is achieved with a de-mixing matrix M^{-1}. With the ICs in W and $M = V \times \sqrt{\Lambda} \times W$:

$$M^{-1} = W^T \frac{1}{\sqrt{\Lambda}} V^T.$$

W and V are orthonormal matrices. Optimizations of ICA algorithms update the matrix of weight vectors $W = (\vec{w}_1, \ldots, \vec{w}_d)$ until convergence. The rotation performed in the white space is expressed by W.

Note that ICA requires the data X to be already whitened. A possible whitening step is e.g. PCA or SVD.

2.4 Dimension Reduction

High-dimensional datasets are reduced to a lower-dimensional space. Two basic approaches address the dimension reduction problem.

Feature Selection. A subset of few – but most meaningful – dimensions from the original dataset are selected.

Feature Extraction. Few novel dimensions are extracted that basically fuse information from many dimensions of the original dataset.

During feature extraction the original data is transformed into a lower-dimensional space. Typically, data transformations, such as SVD, PCA and ICA, are employed. Since these BSS techniques already extract the strongest feature combinations, a back-transformation with truncated source signals e.g. reduces noise from the observed dataset. The feature extraction process may loose information from the observed dataset. But, by definition the dimension reduction via BSS yields new components maintaining a mixture of original dimensions with the most important source information (e.g. variance for PCA or entropy for ICA).

Technically, feature extraction with BSS allows to truncate dimensions in the transformed source space. Source signals (the SV, PC or IC) with low value or little information are removed. In practice, these low scoring values or components may reflect noise fluctuations. By truncating the (noisy) source signals the true underlying sources are maintained. Pruning of the source signals allows to re-transform the signals into the observed data space but resulting in a reduction of dimensions while retaining the data's information content.

2.5 Data Compression

The compression of any type of data is a widely applicable method. For example, the compression of large datasets is indispensable. Compression is simply the encoding of data in fewer bits than its raw representation. But how is the reduction achieved?

2.5.1 Data Communication

An intuitive example helps illustrating the general principle of compression (Figure 2.2). Suppose, we want to transfer data through a communication channel. The sender wants to transfer the string $a^m b^m c$ to the receiver. A naive way would be to transfer each single character requiring in total 16,008 bits for $m = 1,000$ and 8 bits per character. To minimize the communication costs a smart sender exploits regularities in the data. A little program was written which generates the first part of the string by printing 1,000 times the character a followed by 1,000 times b. An efficient coding of the program in an arbitrary programming language requires e.g. 344 bits. The sender additionally transfers c as single character (8 bits) instead of adding a print statement to the little program (which would require e.g. 64 bits). In total, 352 bits are required to transfer the string with the little program. Data compression reduced the communication cost to 2.15% of the naive transmission. Both sender and receiver – the encoder and the decoder – have to be able to understand the transferred code, thus, "speak" the same programming language.

In Figure 2.2, data is compressed in such a way that it is entirely recovered. This lossless compression is only necessary unless a good approximation of the original dataset is sufficient. A lossy compression accepts that a dataset is only decoded with respect to a given precision.

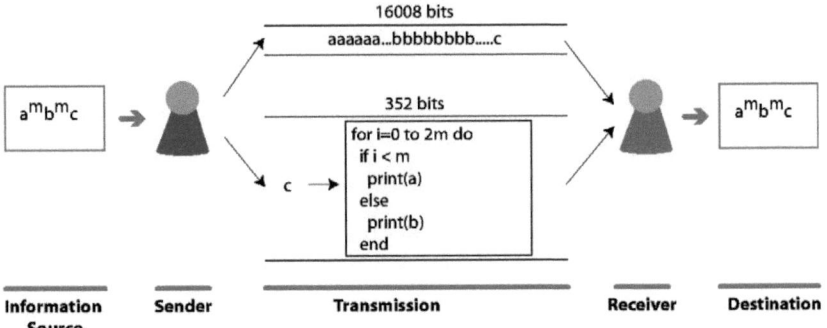

Figure 2.2: Data Communication Scheme. To communicate e.g. a string of $a^m b^m c$ via a communication system, a sender transfers the information on the respective data to a receiver. The receiver has to be able to understand the sender in order to recover the string from the transmitted bits. A crude transmission would be a uncompressed transfer of each single characters one after another. The receiver then just recovers the transferred string by concatenating each received character. A more efficient way to transfer the string is by exploiting the regularities of the string. The information transferred is then a program which the receiver is able to understand (and compile) to thereby recover the string.

2.5 Data Compression

2.5.2 Coding Costs

The procedure to compress a dataset is a search for its regularities in order to find an optimal representation with the shortest possible code (Barron et al. 1998). A crude way to represent numerical data is a maximum-likelihood estimate (Rissanen 1983). To design a good encoding, a Probability Density Function (PDF) is used to imitate the real distribution of the data. Thus, the regularities in the data are identified by estimating its underlying PDF. Frequent data points are well-represented by the PDF and subsequently have short code lengths. As a result, frequent points are strongly compressed.

A strongly compressed data point is consequently cheap with respect to "coding costs". Coding costs represent the costs of transferring any information from sender to receiver. Imagine data points to be drawn from a normal distribution. The regularity then is the underlying normal distribution which is exploited to effectively compress the dataset. For an underlying normal distribution, the PDF parameters mean and standard deviation have also to be estimated and additionally transferred by the sender.

The coding costs c were computed for each single point p in a dataset given one underlying PDF (Figure 2.3). The costs represent how expensive the information transfer of a particular point is. Most frequent data points are imagined to be "regular" and cause little communication costs resulting in cheapest coding costs $c \approx 0$. Whereas "irregular" data points are expensive with $c \gg 0$.

The described principle, that regularity in the dataset may be exploited for compression, is formalized in the MDL principle. MDL, thus, coincides with the corresponding optimization problem to find the optimal code length (Barron et al. 1998).

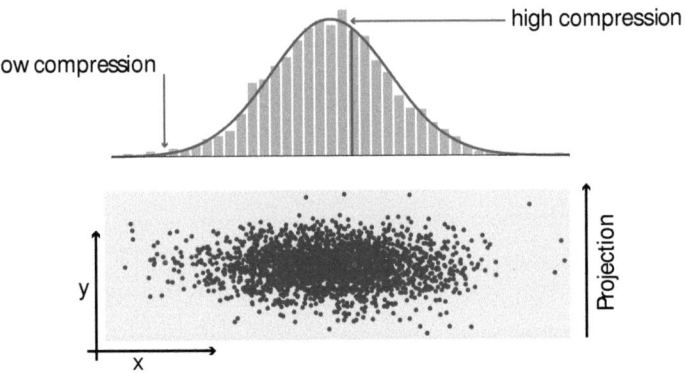

Figure 2.3: Coding costs. When projecting a numerical dataset to one of the axis, the distribution of the points along this axis is determined. A projection of the dataset in y shows that the points are normally distributed in x. Any point frequent with respect to the normal distribution of x-dimension (lilac point and line) is best compressed -- with very low coding costs ($c \to 0$). Any irregular point (highlighted in red) w.r.t. the same normal distribution of x-dimension is poorly compressible, thus has coding costs $c \gg 0$.

2.5 Data Compression

2.5.3 Entropy

To solve the problem to actually find an optimal compression of a dataset, the principle of entropy is consulted from information theory. The entropy H measures how expensive the data transfer actually is. More specifically, H is measuring the uncertainty of the data given known probabilities p_i (Shannon 1948), where p_i is the probability of an object value i to occur. The formula for the entropy, as

$$H(p_i, \ldots, p_n) = -\sum_i p_i \log p_i,$$

coincides with the three demanded properties (Shannon 1948): (1) Continuity in p_i. (2) With all equally likely events ($p_i = 1/n$) uncertainty is maximal. And (3) if one choice is broken in two successive choices H is the weighted sum of the individual H.

For the special case of only two probabilities p and $q = 1 - p$ the distribution of entropy $H(p, q) = -p \log p - q \log q$ is depicted in Figure 2.4. If $p = q = 0.5$ the dataset is generated by chance and is expensive to compress. When using the binary logarithm, the unit of the entropy are bits (Shannon 1948).

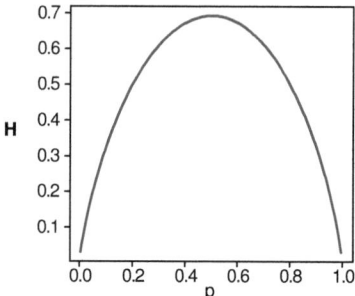

Figure 2.4: Shannon Entropy. Given two probabilities p and $q = 1 - p$ the entropy H is maximal for $p = q = 0.5$.

2.6 Data Mining

To discover knowledge in large dataset manual analysis is not feasible. Knowledge is extracted with techniques from data mining – a process to find hidden information in large datasets. Several concepts and definitions are provided in the following.

Globally and Locally Optimal Solutions. Solutions to a given problem are globally optimal if the solution is the best. When considering the entire solution space – all imaginable solutions to a problem – there are usually many locally optimal solutions where the best solution in the space is the global optimum. If local maxima and minima of the solution space are good and imperfect solutions, a simple "hill-climbing" strategy (each step of the algorithm improves the solution) mostly finds only local optima. Data mining techniques are usually high-climbing techniques, whereas heuristic searches allow to accept worse solutions during runtime in order to find the global optimum.

Objective Function. To numerically evaluate if a given solution to is optimal, objective functions are required. Objective functions are defined for a given problem and provide a measure of goodness of a solution.

Object Similarity. Objects are clustered or classified based on their pairwise similarity. In a numerical vector space, object similarity is usually defined by their spatial distance. Distance functions yield smaller distances for more similar objects. Objects given by categorical attributes are more similar the more attributes they have in common.

Clustering. Clustering algorithms find a grouping or ordering of objects in the dataset. Intrinsic dataset structures are revealed.

Heuristics. For complex problems which are not solvable in a reasonable amount of time by an exhaustive search or standard data mining strategies, various heuristic strategies are used. Heuristic strategies provide a good solution to a complex problem, but have usually high runtimes. Instead of a hill-climbing strategy, heuristics explore the search space by also accepting intermediate solution which are worse than those already evaluated.

2.6.1 K-means Clustering

K-means clustering was initially proposed to cluster data points in space, given a specific distance measure (Macqueen 1967). The dataset was partitioned into exactly k clusters, each represented by a cluster representative, the mean value of the data points associated to the cluster. This distance based clustering is a basic technique for minimizing variances.

The k-means algorithm iterates until convergence by first calculating all k cluster representative and then reassigning the data points to the closest cluster representative. By assigning each point to the closest cluster representative, cluster variances are subsequently minimized. Two approaches of the k-means algorithms were proposed where the update of the cluster representative(s) is computed either after one data point changes its cluster membership (Macqueen 1967) or after all data points are again assigned to its closest representative (Lloyd 1982). Convergence is reached if no chances in the cluster composition occurred.

2.6.2 Evaluation Measures

Modularity

Modularity was initially introduced as a measure of community structure (Newman and Girvan 2004) for a graph $G = (V, E)$. It measures how modular a set of nodes is compared to a random network model with identical connectivity. The fraction of edges between cluster i and cluster j is corrected for the connectivity of the individual clusters.

Following Newman and Girvan (2004), modularity is defined by the matrix $F = (f_{ij})$ holding the fractions of edges that connect the clusters. For a graph partitioned into k clusters $\dim(F) = k \times k$. The entries f_{ij} are the fraction of edges of the graph connecting vertices of modules i and j. The matrix F is not sufficient to quantify community structure since row and column sums have to be considered as well: The overall connectivity of the cluster i is the degree sum of all vertices in i – or $a_i = \sum_j f_{ij}$. The modularity Q of a given community structure is

$$Q = Tr\, F - \|F^2\| = \sum_i (f_{ij} - a_i^2)$$

with $\|F^2\|$ the sum of squared entries of F.

Modularity Q may be reformulated as a function of the absolute number (not fractions) of l_i the number of links enclosed by the cluster i and d_i the sum of the degree of the nodes of cluster i. Furthermore, $L = |E|$ and resulting $2L = 2|E| = \sum_i d_i$. As a result, Q is calculated also from (Guimera and Nunes Amaral 2005, Guimera et al. 2004)

$$Q = \sum_{c=1}^{k} \left(\frac{l_c}{L} - \left(\frac{d_c}{2L} \right)^2 \right).$$

In more detail, a_i is the probability of randomly picking one edge that leads to community i. Following, a_i^2 is the probability that both ends of one edge lead to community i, which is nothing else than the expected value for a randomly connected network with same community partition. In other words, $a_i^2 = (d_i/2L)^2$ approximates the fraction of links to be expect by chance to have both connecting nodes inside the same module, assuming self-links and multiple links between nodes are not allowed.

2.6 Data Mining

Extending the modularity measure to a symmetric modularity matrix $M = (m_{ij})$, the matrix entries are defined by

$$m_{ij} = f_{ij} - \frac{d_i d_j}{2L}$$

where d_i is the degree sum of all nodes in cluster i and $2L = \sum_i d_i$ (Newman 2006).

Statistical Enrichment

To assess if a set of objects over-represents one characteristic with respect to the background set of all available objects, the calculation of the respective percentage is not sufficient. For statistical meaningful values, the hypergeometric distribution is employed to determine the statical enrichment of one characteristic of an object subset compared to the background objects.

The number of all objects of the background (or database, or population) is N, out of which a subset of size n was selected. The objects are characterized by one attribute, which is either present or not (e.g. white and black=non-white balls in a jar). The number of all objects with the characteristic is M, while the number of objects with the characteristic in the subset is m. Thus, $N \geq M$ and $n \geq m$. The probability that *at least those m objects* have the characteristic in the subset is defined as

$$\text{p-value} = \sum_{i=m}^{n} \frac{\binom{M}{i}\binom{N-M}{n-i}}{\binom{N}{n}} = 1 - \sum_{i=0}^{m-1} \frac{\binom{M}{i}\binom{N-M}{n-i}}{\binom{N}{n}}$$

For example, the hypergeometric distribution is transferrable to determine whether a set of proteins is statistically enriched for a specific protein function with respect to the underlying *proteome*. The entire *proteome* is clustered into k clusters. The question arises, if the enrichment of e.g. the kinase activity of the proteins in one cluster $1 \leq j \leq k$ is significantly enriched. Of all proteins with the kinase function in the *proteome* (M) the number of proteins with kinase function in cluster j (m) are counted, in addition to the size of the jth cluster (n) and the size of the proteome (N). The resulting p-value is calculated to determine if the enrichment is significant.

If objects are characterized by more than one attribute the enrichment is subsequently calculated for each attribute under the assumption that the remaining attributes are identical. Since this trick in turn induces a huge statistical bias, multiple testing has to be performed to correct significance levels.

The enrichment is typically calculated for a Gene Ontology term, when analyzing clusters in a *interactome* (Brohee et al. 2008, Bu et al. 2003, Cho et al. 2007) or a differential transcriptome (Boyle et al. 2004). The enrichment of differentially expressed KEGG pathways was performed in Gormanns et al. (2011).

2.7 Related Algorithms

2.7.1 Data Transformation

AMUSE

AMUSE performs ICA with basically two consecutive eigenvalue decompositions (Tong et al. 1990, for the details). First, SVD of the estimated covariance of X is performed and the singular values ($\psi_1, \ldots \psi_m$) are used to transform X via $y = CX$ with $C = \text{diag}(1/\psi_1, \ldots 1/\psi_m)$ into the white space. Second, From a derivative $((R_y(\tau) + R_y(\tau)^T)/2)$ of the autocorrelation matrix R_y another SVD is performed yielding again singular values in V. Finally, source signals and the mixing matrix are estimated with $\hat{s} = V^T C x$ and $A = U_s \text{diag}(\psi_i \ldots \psi_m) V$, respectively.

2.7 Related Algorithms

FastICA

FastICA is a fast fix-point algorithm to perform ICA (Hyvarinen 1999, for the details). Starting with maximization of the first IC and iteratively optimizing for the remaining ICs one-by-one, FastICA uses information theory to calculate $s = WX$. By exploiting mutual information as an information theoretic measure of independence, the mutual information of transformed components s_i is minimized. The principle of negentropy $J(W)$ of differential entropies is used as contrast function for finding the ICs. $J(y) = H(y_{gauss}) - H(y)$ gets maximized, with y_{gauss} being a Gaussian random vector of same covariance as y and $H(y) = \int f(y) \log f(y) dy$. PCA may be used to whiten the raw data X prior to the fix-point iterations estimating W. Potential dimension reduction is implemented by finding only a limited number of ICs, thus interrupting the one-by-one IC maximization step.

SOBI

SOBI is based on second order information during a joint diagonalization step of a set of correlation matrices (Belouchrani et al. 1993, for the details). The white space transformation is performed via the covariance matrix of X. Of the whitened data a set of whitened covariance matrix of different time lags are computed. Their joint diagonalization enables a robust estimate of a sound unitary matrix to calculate the estimate of the source signals. Potential dimension reduction is implemented by already reducing the dimensionality of the white space, thus through the step of decomposing the sample covariance matrix.

2.7.2 Graph Clustering

Markov Clustering

The Markov Cluster algorithm (MCL) is a popular algorithm used in life sciences for fast clustering of weighted graphs. MCL basically identifies high-flow regions as clusters in a weighted graph (Stijn 2000). An inflation parameter alters the steps used to separate weak and strong flow regions. Consequently, the inflation parameter determines the granularity of the resulting clusters, thus influences k.

Metis

Metis is a class of well-known multi-level partitioning techniques. (Karypis and Kumar 1998a,b,c). For graph partitioning a sequence of successively smaller (coarser) graphs is constructed and a bisection of the coarsest graph is computed. Then the bisection is successively brought to the level of a finer graph, and at each level an iterative refinement algorithm is used to further improve the bisection. A more robust multilevel paradigm was introduced (Karypis and Kumar 1998b) which presented a powerful graph coarsening scheme where even a good bisection of the coarsest graph is a good bisection of the original graph. It also allows the usage of simplified variants to speed up the refinement without compromising the overall quality. The number of k clusters has to be set for Metis.

MDL-based Clustering of Unweighted Graphs

The Cross-Association clustering algorithm has to be mentioned for completeness. Similar to *PaCCo*, Cross-Association finds groups in (bipartite) unweighted graphs by lossless compression with MDL in a parameter-free algorithm (Deepayan et al. 2004). Although the algorithm is not explicitly designed for just bipartite graphs, the meaningful interpretation of off-diagonal clusters (where one object might be at the same time inside and

2.7 Related Algorithms

outside one cluster, depending if rows or column groups are considered) is rather intriguing. However, the idea of using MDL for clustering served as inspiring example for the *PaCCo* algorithm.

Spectral Clustering

Spectral clustering refers to a class of techniques which relies on the eigenstructure of a similarity matrix in order to partition objects into disjoint clusters. It is a well-known partitioning technique for similarity matrices. The objective function minimizes the normalized cut commonly achieved by eigen decompositions. The algorithm proposed by Ng et al. (2001) detects arbitrarily shaped clusters by considering the clustering problem from a graph-theoretic perspective. A cluster is obtained by removing the weakest edges between highly connected subgraphs. Another algorithm is a learning method (Jordan and Bach 2003) to derive a new cost function based on a measure of error between a given partition and a solution of the spectral relaxation of a minimum normalized cut problem.

Similar to k-means (Macqueen 1967), the problem of most spectral clustering approaches is the choice of a suitable number of k clusters. In addition, they are sensitive to outliers, i.e. noise in the similarity matrix. To overcome the difficulty of selecting the suitable number of clusters Zelnik-Manor and Perona (2004) proposed a spectral clustering method which investigates the structure of the eigenvectors to infer the number of clusters.

For a detailed tutorial on spectral clustering refer to von Luxburg (2007).

2.7.3 Outlier Detection

The most established approaches to outlier detection in databases are classified into the two categories of distance- and density-based approaches. For an extended survey on anomaly detection please refer to Varun et al. (2009).

Density-based Outlier Detection

Density-based outlier detection introduces an outlier notion derived from density-based clustering and, therefore, detects not only global but also local outliers. A point is flagged as an outlier if it does not fit well into the objects neighborhood density.

LOCI. LOCI is a density-based multi-granularity outlier factor (Papadimitriou et al. 2003). Points are regarded as outliers if the object density in their local neighborhood deviates significantly from the average object density in the local neighborhood. The local neighborhood is specified by two parameters, which are called counting and sampling neighborhood. The counting neighborhood specifies some volume of the feature space which is used to estimate the local object density. The sampling neighborhood is larger than the counting neighborhood and contains all points which are used to compute the average object density in the neighborhood. LOCI is featured by this decoupling of counting and sampling neighborhoods. It can be demonstrated that without this decoupling, density estimation leads to incorrect results in some specific cases. In addition, the decoupling enables an efficient computation of LOCI. However, the decoupling requires the specification of additional parameters. Together with the outlier factor, the LOCI approach proposes a visualization, the so-called LOCI plot which displays the LOCI of a point with respect to increasing sizes of the local neighborhood and, thereby, allows e.g. to identify micro-clusters. LOCI uses the Euclidean distance as a global

2.7 Related Algorithms

metric distance function. In addition, the LOCI approach proposes to flag points as outliers which deviate in their local object density more than three times of the standard deviation of the overall object density of the sampling neighborhood. This flagging assumes a Gaussian distribution of the object densities.

LOF. The Local Outlier Factor (LOF) formalizes the idea of density-based outlier detection by considering the MinPts nearest neighbors of an object as its neighborhood (Breunig et al. 2000). The LOF of an object is defined by the ratio of its MinPts-nearest neighbor distance and the mean MinPts-nearest neighbor distance in its neighborhood. However, the global parameter MinPts strongly affects the outlier detection result: Arbitrary high or low values of MinPts either regard small cluster points as outliers or do not detect outliers, respectively. LOF approach applies an Euclidean distance metric to identify outliers.

Distance-based Outlier Detection

Distance-based outlier detection is among the earliest approaches and has been proposed and further elaborated by Knorr and Ng (1997, 1998, 1999). An object o of a database DB is a distance-based outlier if at least a fraction β of the objects in DB have a distance greater than a previously specified distance d. This basic approach provides binary flagging of points as outliers or non-outliers. An extension (Knorr and Ng 1999) proposes to support semantic interpretation of distance-based outliers. However, without knowledge of the data distribution, it is difficult to specify suitable values for the parameters β and d. In addition, a fixed distance threshold d identifies only global outliers.

Minimum Description Length in Data Mining

Information-theoretic concepts, especially the MDL principle and related ideas, have been recently successfully applied to clustering (Böhm et al. 2006, 2008, Pelleg and Moore 2000), and are also established in the areas of regression (Robnik-Sikonja and Kononenko 1998), rule mining (Yoshida et al. 2002), classification (Kim and Kweon 2006) and anomaly detection (Keogh et al. 2004). The MDL principle relates learning and data compression. Learning regularities from data allows to compress the data more efficiently. For model selection in clustering and classification, MDL allows to compare different candidate models achieving a natural balance between goodness of fit and model complexity. To the best of our knowledge, the MDL principle was first applied to the problem of outlier detection by *CoCo*.

Regarding the problem specification, clustering is most related to outlier detection. But outliers are regarded as a problem for clustering, since they may severely affect the result of most algorithms. A parameter-free extension of K-means clustering is X-Means (Pelleg and Moore 2000). However, the X-Means algorithm is restricted to spherical Gaussian clusters and very sensitive to outliers. RIC (Böhm et al. 2006) has been designed as a post-processing step to improve an initial clustering of an arbitrary conventional clustering algorithm. After filtering the initial clusters from noise, for each cluster a model is determined. This model comprises a rotation matrix determined by PCA and a PDF assigned to each coordinate selected from a set of predefined PDFs. The recently proposed algorithm OCI (Böhm et al. 2008) introduces a very general clustering notion based on the EPD and ICA. Also related are approaches to MDL-based de-noising of signals (Rissanen 2000, Xie et al. 2004). However, these approaches are especially designed for time series and their goal is to reconstruct the signal as accurate as possible.

3 Shared Features in Weighted Graphs

Object similarities are now more and more characterized by connectivity information available in form of networks. Complex graph datasets arose from various fields, like e-commerce, social networks and high-throughput biology. The obtained information characterizing the object interactions was often not binary but rather associated with interaction strengths. Edges of the resulting graphs subsequently possessed numeric weights. The grouping of highly connected nodes is an important task and allowed to extract valuable knowledge from the entire dataset. Many popular clustering techniques were designed for unweighted graphs but were not be directly applicable to weighted graphs. To this end, we have proposed a novel clustering algorithm for weighted graphs, called *PaCCo* (PArameter-free Clustering by COding costs), which is based on the Minimum Description Length (MDL) principle coupled to a bisecting k-means strategy. The MDL principle allowed to relate the clustering problem to the problem of data compression: A good graph cluster structure enabled strong graph compression. The compression efficiency depended on the underlying edge weights constituting the graph connectivity. The compression rate served as similarity or distance metric between the nodes. Furthermore, the MDL principle ensured that the algorithm was parameter free and automatically found the number of clusters. Restrictive assumptions were bypassed and no *a priori* information on the network was required. We systematically evaluated the clustering approach *PaCCo* on synthetic as well as on *interactome* data to demonstrate the superiority of the developed algorithm over existing approaches.

The part of this chapter on *PaCCo* was published with equal contribution of Katrin Haegler in Müller et al. (2011a).

3.1 Biological Question and Data

3.1.1 Interactomes

Interactomics is the study of molecular interaction profiles of organisms. Molecular interactions on protein level were distinguished by their type: Two or more proteins interact physically by forming direct physical contacts via e.g. chemical bonds; Two or more proteins genetically interact when deletion or knock-down of their protein-encoding genes severely altered the wild type (wt) phenotype. Although the deletion occurred on genetic level, interaction knowledge on protein level was inferred since the encoded proteins were those molecules eventually affecting the organisms' phenotype. Retrieved data was accumulated in graphs yielding the protein-protein interaction (PPI) networks. Since the development of PPI high-throughput screenings, the number of edges has been increasing while the number of proteins per organism has stayed more or less constant. Analyses of PPI networks retrieved and even helped to predict e.g. protein complexes (Collins et al. 2007, Sprinzak et al. 2006) and molecular functions of unknown proteins (Carter et al. 2009, Holme and Huss 2005, Song and Singh 2009).

Physical interactions were identified in a high-throughput manner with approaches screening whether interactions were generally possible (e.g. with yeast two-hybrid or tandem affinity purification coupled to Mass Spectrometry (MS) (Gavin et al. 2002)) or screening for interactions in the native protein environments (e.g. protein complementation assay (Tarassov et al.

2008)). All approaches yielded yes-or-no interaction values generating binary dataset of unweighted graphs. To generate weighted graphs of physical PPI, their edges may be assigned to uncertainty values assessing the probability that the interaction was technically correct. The number of how many times an interaction was measured by different approaches may also be used as weight (Pinkert et al. 2010). A general measure of interaction strength was not available.

Genetic interactions, in contrast, were quantified by interaction strength. The standard approach to screen for genetic interactions was a Synthetic Genetic Assay (SGA) where interaction strength was quantified by organism fitness (Tong et al. 2004). SGA methods were developed for the model organism yeast for *genome* subsets (Schuldiner et al. 2005, 2006) as well as for the entire *genome* (Boone et al. 2007). Experimentally, the SGA design was driven by the concept that growth of yeast colonies are significantly reduced or increased, if cells have fitness defects or benefits, respectively, as a result of two deleted genes. In the extreme case where organisms with a double gene knockout were not viable, the two genes were called to be synthetic lethal. The interpretation of a synthetic lethal interaction was not a functional redundancy but rather a severe effect on two parallel pathways (Tischler et al. 2008). Therein, deletion of the first gene induced molecular rearrangements of pathways inducing lethality on a second gene. Genetic PPI networks were undirected weighted graphs offering a new level of complexity for biological evaluation which has to be met with new techniques.

3.1.2 Interactome Clustering

network of PPI required especial attention during analysis and their evaluation was challenging (Beyer et al. 2007). Not every PPI dataset should be used right away for analysis, but effort has to be made to verify experimental confidence (Collins et al. 2007). Several public databases already integrated published PPI across organisms and methods (Guldener et al.

2006, Stark et al. 2006, as examples)), however, the analysis of physical and genetic PPI graphs has always to be handled independently. Solely results allowed integration across their interaction types.

Most clustering of PPI networks – the organism's *interactome* – was performed on binary graphs assembled from physical interactions (Guimera and Nunes Amaral 2005, Hwang et al. 2006, Luo et al. 2007, Newman and Girvan 2004). Only few clustering algorithms were be applied to weighted PPI networks, such as MCL (Stijn 2000) and spectral clustering algorithms (Bu et al. 2003, Newman 2006). Comparisons and reviews on several clustering results for PPI highlighted benefits and drawbacks with respect to biological problems (Andreopoulos et al. 2009, Brohee and van Helden 2006). While spectral clustering and MCL were both widely used, spectral clustering algorithms were not efficient resulting in high runtimes and MCL was very parameter-dependent (Andreopoulos et al. 2009). For clustering of PPI, the concept of modularity played a large role to measure the clustering degree (Girvan and Newman 2002, Guimera and Nunes Amaral 2005, Newman 2006, Newman and Girvan 2004, Vinogradov 2008). Novel graph clustering algorithms have to be benchmarked by their robustness to noise and outlier (Andreopoulos et al. 2009).

3.1.3 The Yeast Synthetic Lethal Interactome

The real dataset used for our graph clustering study was originated from high-throughput biology. Pairwise deletions of always two yeast genes were interrogated for fitness effects. The only organism-wide synthetic lethal screen published was used as sample for our study (Costanzo et al. 2010). The highly interconnected synthetic *interactome* contained 1,139 nodes (the proteins) and 13,452 edges (Figure 3.1a). Simultaneous deletion of two genes increased (positive) or decreased (negative) colony growth (if at all) and yielded edge weights of positive and negative values. Growth rates above 0.15 epsilon score were selected (Figure 3.1b).

3.1 Biological Question and Data

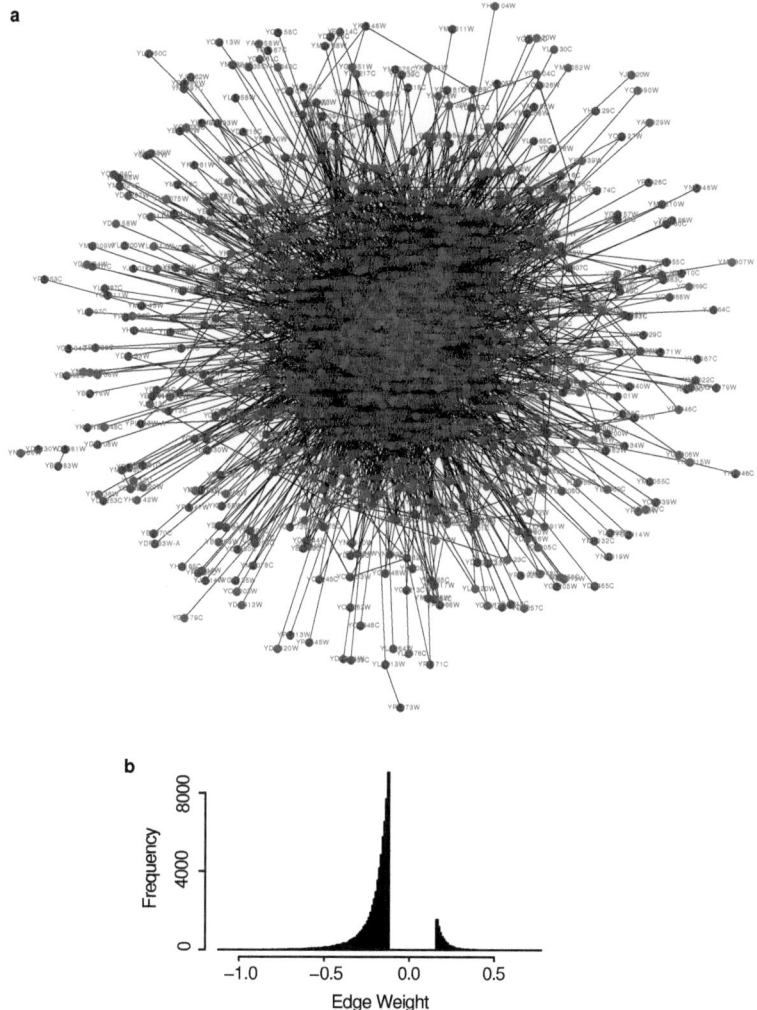

Figure 3.1: Yeast Synthetic Lethal *Interactome*. a. Graph of genetic interaction screen in yeast. Nodes are labeled with systematic gene names. Node color is gradually changing from red to blue indicating their cluster membership. **a*.** When clustered with SA extension for weighted graphs, 1084 clusters were identified and the cluster membership of each node was color coded by a gradient. Most clusters were singletons and the largest clusters contained at most 2 nodes. **b.** Histogram of of all edge weights.

3.2 Weighted Graph Clustering with Simulated Annealing

3.2.1 Simulated Annealing Algorithm

Initial Algorithm Core

The computation of a globally optimal graph clustering is generally very expensive. To cope with expensive computation costs, the heuristic of simulated annealing (SA) was developed (Cerny 1985, Kirkpatrick et al. 1983). Algorithm 3.1 provides an outline to the problem solution already adapted to graph clustering, following Guimera and Nunes Amaral (2005). SA was based on two basic ideas: First, the current solution was randomly altered to small extends. Second, a computational temperature was introduced to accept random changes more frequently by chance when the "temperature was high". The more the "system cools down" during runtime only changes improving the solution were accepted. As a result, the heuristic design allowed to explore the solution space with help of the computational temperature.

Algorithm 3.1 Graph Clustering with Simulated Annealing
---
    initiate random clustering with costs C_c
    while computational temperature (t) > 0 **do**
        loop
            randomly permute the cluster set
            calculate the costs of permuted cluster set (C_n)
            if $C_n > C_c$ **or** $\exp(-((C_n - C_c)/t)) \geq$ random number **then**
                accept permuted clustering $(C_c = C_n)$
            end if
        end loop
        cool temperature t
    end while
    return C_c

3.2 Weighted Graph Clustering with Simulated Annealing

Figure 3.2 depicts a minimal example of graph clustering principle with SA derived from Guimera and Nunes Amaral (2005). Clusters were initialized by assigning each node in the graph to an individual cluster (Figure 3.2a). Clusters containing solely one node were "singletons". Random permutations of the current clustering altered node cluster memberships: Either a single node or a collective movement was performed. Within one temperature level, Individual node movements were selected more frequently ($|V|^2$ times) than collective movements ($|V|$ times) to sample the cluster memberships. For moving a single node from one cluster to another, a node was randomly drawn and then reassigned to another random cluster. For moving a set of nodes in a collective manner, a random cluster was drawn and either split into two clusters of random size or merged with another random cluster. When plotting the runtime versus current costs of the present clustering structure, clustering costs tended to fluctuate more for higher temperatures (Figure 3.2b). During low temperature stages, SA optimized the clustering solution with a simple hill-climbing character. The obtained graph clustering yielded a globally optimal solution (Figure 3.2c).

SA Extension for Weighted Graphs

The cost evaluation function of the SA graph clustering was modularity. Modularity was also widely used as quality function (Danon et al. 2005, Fortunato 2010, Girvan and Newman 2002). and initially proposed to favor inner-cluster connectivity above random. Edges inside a cluster were maximized (inter-cluster edges) while simultaneously minimizing edges between clusters (intra-cluster edges). Formally, modularity on a graph partitioning of an unweighted graph into k clusters was

$$Q = \sum_{c=1}^{k} \left(\frac{l_c}{L} - \left(\frac{d_c}{2L} \right)^2 \right)$$

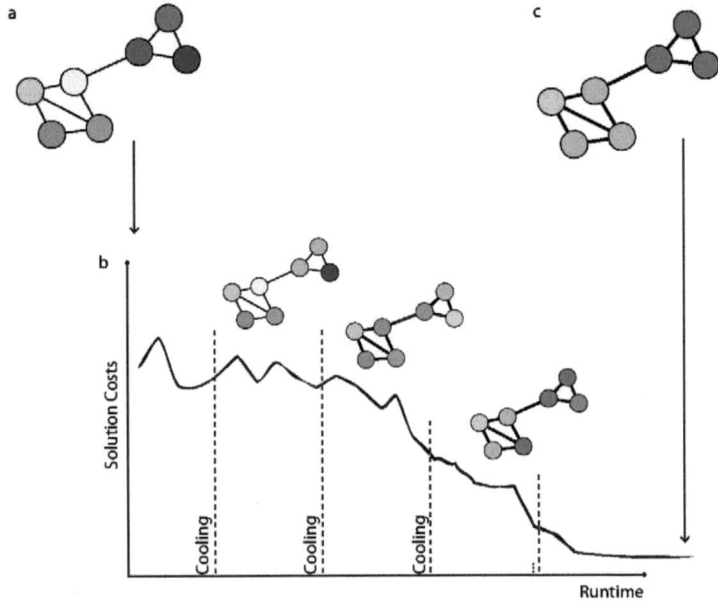

Figure 3.2: Simulated Annealing for Graph Clustering. Sketching SA snapshots during runtime. **a.** Graph to be clustered. Nodes are color-coded by cluster membership. Initiation of SA graph clustering with singleton clusters. **b.** Runtime of SA explores solution space. Costs of intermediate clustering is visualized at current runtime. Corresponding potential solutions of the graph color-coded accordingly. Temperature cooling steps are indicated by dotted line. **c.** Globally optimal clustering result of the graph.

3.2 Weighted Graph Clustering with Simulated Annealing

with $L = |V|$ being the number of all edges inside the graph, l_c the number of links enclosed by the cluster c, and d_c the degree sum of nodes in cluster c. Edge enclosed by one cluster linked two nodes within the same cluster. This definition for unweighted graphs was originally used for SA clustering (Guimera and Nunes Amaral 2005) but was not applicable to weighted graphs, unless weighted graph was thresholded. Binarization of weighted graphs approximated true clustering only roughly. Instead, a weighted modularity definition would allow to compute the exact modularity based on the exact weights.

To enable clustering of weighted graphs with SA, we redefined modularity to account for edge weights. A straight-forward extension substituted the binary edge-or-no-edge information with edge weights. Edge weights were considered instead of the edge counts by using W as the sum of all weights (substituting L), w_c as weights enclosed by cluster c (substituting l_s) as well as d_{w_c} as the weighted degree of all nodes inside cluster c (substituting d_c). We subsequently defined weighted modularity like

$$Q_w = \sum_{c=1}^{k} \left(\frac{w_c}{W} - \left(\frac{d_{w_c}}{2W} \right)^2 \right).$$

3.2.2 Performance on Interactome

We clustered the genome-wide synthetic lethal *interactome* of yeast with the weighted graph clustering extension of the SA algorithm of Guimera and Nunes Amaral (2005). The clustering result yielded 1084 clusters with a weighted modularity of Q_w = 0.06811 (Figure 3.1a*). Given the number of 1139 nodes in the *interactome* the fine-grained fragmentation into almost only single-node clusters, we concluded that graph clustering with SA was sufficient to generate a meaningful clustering.

3.3 Improved Weighted Graph Clustering with PaCCo

To illustrate the desired result of a weighted graph clustering, we used a simplified example: Weighted graph clustering started with a rather confusing network and revealed an underlying simpler graph structure (Figure 3.3). The nodes assigned to the same cluster were placed in close proximity to better illustrate the clustering process. Nodes were colored with respect to cluster membership and edges with respect to their weights. Note, that each final cluster contained edges with similar weights (low, medium and high edge weights for the three clusters). This emphasized that the clustering process should not only minimize the number of edges between clusters but also maximize weight similarity of clusters.

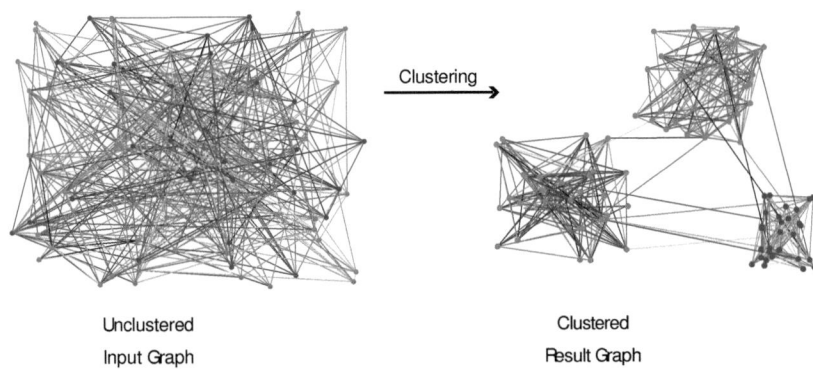

Figure 3.3: Weighted Graph Clustering Example. Clustering of a weighted graph maximized the number of edges inside each cluster while minimizing edges between clusters. Edge weights were colored in gray with respect to their weights (dark gray for high weights). Nodes got colored with respect to their cluster identity. Nodes with similar cluster identity were grouped for illustration purposes.

3.3 Improved Weighted Graph Clustering with PaCCo

3.3.1 Motivation

Large-scale technologies generated huge amounts of data on an every day basis. The first steps towards the understanding of underlying patterns was the identification of meaningful subgroups. In order to extract this invaluable information subdivision of a dataset into two or more partitions was based on object similarity measures without knowing where to subdivide the dataset. This clustering procedure was very complex when data was saved in a network format: Objects to be clustered were nodes with node-to-node edge information determining the similarity or linkage between one another.

Organism-wide PPI networks or social connectivity in social networks were easily and often quickly obtained, but their interpretation was rather difficult. Beyond single node statistics on graphs, the quantification of object relationships represented a challenging task but eventually revealed clusters of similar nodes. Graph partitioning split the set of nodes into non-overlapping meaningful subsets of highly interlinked nodes. The edges in the graph served as node-to-node similarity information used by the clustering algorithm. Considering not only whether two nodes were connected or not, the strength of the connection (represented as edge weights) added additional information to node similarities. The edge weight information contributed to graph clusters and had to be separately handled by the clustering algorithm. If edge weights are neglected through binarization by thresholding, the true graph clusters cannot be revealed but at most roughly approximated.

Nodes belonging to one cluster were assumed to either share similar interest, e.g. mobile users in a social network, or similar function, e.g. proteins in a PPI network. With the help of clustering techniques the prediction of e.g. protein function of an unknown protein was feasible by identifying functionally homogeneous clusters based on known proteins. The continuous similarity information between proteins provided more biologically relevant information than simple "zero-or-one" interactions. Thus, the weighted clustering revealed functional classes which were e.g. biologically more reliable. With respect to social networks, based on calling behaviors from mobile phone companies, groups of common interest were identified. For example, people strongly interacting with a group of iPhone-users were more likely to buy an iPhone as well.

Real datasets and graph models were well-described with respect to graph connectivities. The standard graph model assumptions were random, scale-free and hierarchical distribution characterized by a unique combination of node degree and clustering coefficient distribution (Barabasi and Oltvai 2004). Real-world data was usually said to be a scale-free network, but more and more datasets to date did not follow any of the three initial distributions (Higham et al. 2008, e.g. PPI fitted to a geometric graph). Looking at weight distributions of real-world datasets no general rules were found or evaluated so far. Indeed, already in biological sciences the weight distributions differed depending on kind of edge weight information.

We presented a novel parameter-free and fully automatic weighted graph clustering approach, called *PaCCo* (Müller et al. 2011a). Data compression principle with MDL enabled efficiently clustering of weighted graphs into meaningful subgraphs. By iteratively splitting clusters into subclusters until a split compressed the graph not any further, we not only produced accurate results but also saved computational time when compared to existing graph clustering methods. Our major contributions were:

Parameter-free: *PaCCo* required no user specific parameter settings (like e.g. number of clusters of the dataset) in order to find meaningful clustering results.

Fully automatic: Entirely automatic, *PaCCo* required no intervention from the user since we used MDL principle also as convergence criterion.

3.3 Improved Weighted Graph Clustering with PaCCo

Reduced runtime: The top-down splitting approach of *PaCCo* saved computational time while keeping high clustering accuracy. *PaCCo* runtime was comparable to parameter-dependent methods.

Current problems in graph mining algorithms were the selection of parameters, scalability, and runtime (Schaeffer 2007). In addition, evaluation of graph clustering results was an important and difficult issue that had also to be addressed by novel graph clustering algorithms. We addressed the problem of parameter settings by consistently using the principle of data compression for clustering without any *a priori* knowledge of the data. The idea of data compression was based on the identification of regularities of a dataset and using these regularities for efficient compression. The MDL principle was a method from information theory to measure regularities in data (Rissanen 1983), consequently, more regular data were better compressed than irregular data. Thus, we employed graph compression as sole objective function for clustering.

3.3.2 Designing Novel PaCCo Algorithm

To cope with the shortcomings of current weighted graph clustering algorithms, we have developed a parameter-free clustering algorithm based on coding costs, short *PaCCo*. *PaCCo* clustered nodes in a weighted graph by combining a bisecting k-means (Macqueen 1967) strategy with the principle of data compression. In a top-down splitting approach *PaCCo* used data compression not only to automatically find the number of clusters in a graph but also to reassign nodes to their most similar cluster. As data compression strategy we applied the MDL principle to evaluate the goodness of clusterings.

Data compression allowed to infer costs of a graph clustering. A good clustering of a graph G led to a strong graph compression which was in turn equivalent to low coding costs. Consequently, the graph clustering algorithm of *PaCCo* had to minimize the coding costs of a graph partitioning $C = \{C_1, ..., C_k\}$ caused by the k clusters and their parameters. The model costs, that arose when transferring information on any graph clustering, were calculated for a graph G given a clustering C as

$$\text{Model-Cost}(G|C) = \sum_{l=1}^{k} c(C_l) + c(p).$$

The total model costs took not only costs of all clusters $c(C_l)$ into account, but also compression costs of the cluster model $c(p)$ itself. The parameter costs of p corrected the overall costs for cluster model complexity depending on of the number of clusters.

PaCCo was able to find a graph clustering using solely an undirected weighted graph as input. Clusters to be identified were highly interlinked subgraphs with similar weights with minimal links between clusters. In general, *PaCCo* algorithm was a two-step minimization of the model costs with

1. Graph splitting and

2. Graph clustering using *k-PaCCo*.

The graph splitting step bisected any (sub)graph while the clustering step with *k-PaCCo* evolved the subgraph clusterings. In detail, *k-PaCCo* used a k-means strategy as an algorithmic scaffold to assign the nodes to k clusters by minimizing the model costs. Model costs were furthermore used as the convergence criterion to stop the splitting process.

As a visual outline, Figure 3.4 depicts a sample run of *PaCCo*. Within a top-down bisecting strategy, the graph (given as adjacency matrix) was iteratively split into two subgraphs whenever a split "payed off". Starting with the entire graph, *PaCCo* tried to split the input graph using *k-PaCCo* with $k = 2$ until convergence. In the following we referred to the *k-PaCCo* routine with $k = 2$ as "*2-PaCCo*". Lower coding costs indicated improved data compression, consequently the resulting subclustering was more accu-

3.3 Improved Weighted Graph Clustering with PaCCo

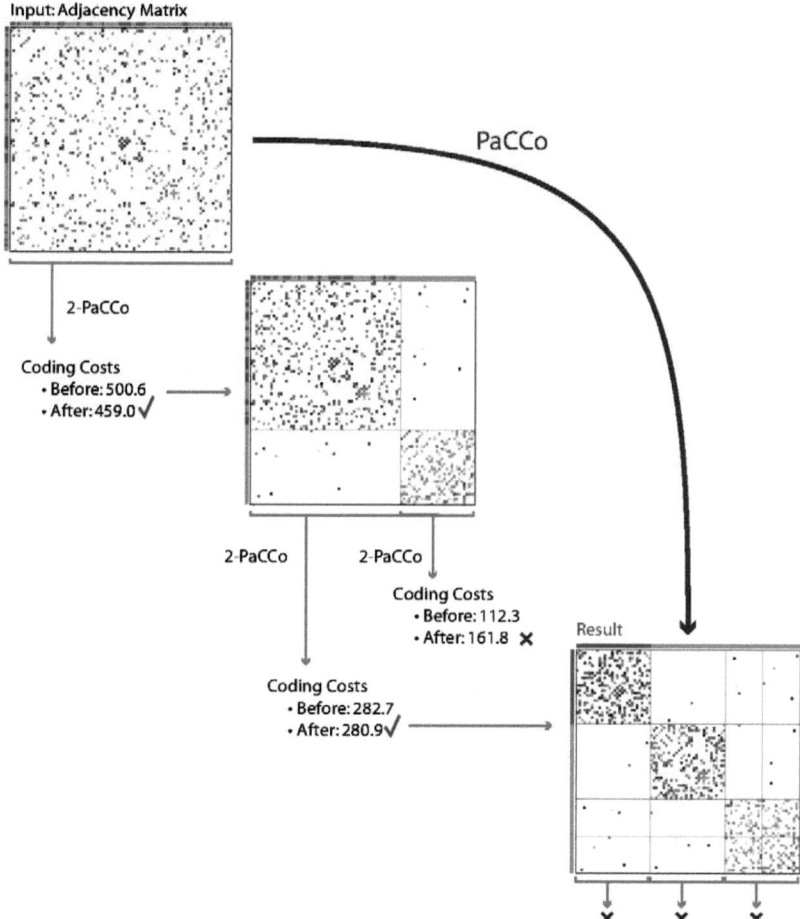

Figure 3.4: *PaCCo* Weighted Graph Clustering Design. Only the adjacency matrix of a graph was used as input. The matrix contained continuous weight information as node-to-node similarities. Iteratively the subroutine *k-PaCCo* was called with $k=2$ to split the (sub-)graph. The coding costs were calculated to determine the graph compression. If coding costs) were lower after the *k-PaCCo* splitting, then the split was accepted, otherwise rejected and added as final cluster in the clustering C. Nodes were colored in pink, green and blue according to their cluster membership. Clusters were blocks along the diagonal and split lines are drawn where cluster membership changes.

rate. Thus, if the model costs were lower after the 2-*PaCCo* run, the (sub-)graph split was accepted. Each subgraph was subsequently handled separately, whereby, 2-*PaCCo* was once again applied to each. Finally, *PaCCo* converged when coding costs of every already accepted cluster was cheaper than its split version. In the end, the adjacency matrix was restructured by equally reordering the rows and columns with respect to the clustering result.

3.3.3   PaCCo Algorithm Design

PaCCo began the graph clustering with an undirected weighted graph and identified the number of clusters without knowing the true value of k. The algorithm followed a basic recursive concept (Algorithm 3.2). The initial adjacency matrix A was used as single input to the algorithm. In order to get a first information on the entire input graph weights, we initialized the clustering with a k-*PaCCo* step using $k = 1$. Especially, information on the weight distribution of the entire graph offered a cluster initialization which was better-than-random. This initiation step required only one iteration until convergence (since the cluster membership never changes). With this first calculation we obtained an initialization of the top cluster which was better than random. The graph was subsequently bisected in a top-down manner whereby the final clustering result V was tracked. The final result inherently contained the number of k clusters in the graph.

3.3.4   PaCCo Cluster Representatives

Graph and Cluster Notion

Let $G = (V, E)$ be an undirected weighted graph with a set of $n = |V|$ nodes and a set of $|E|$ edges, whereby, the undirected edge $e_{ij} = e_{ji}$ indicated a connection between the nodes v_i and v_j. Furthermore, let G be stored in

3.3 Improved Weighted Graph Clustering with PaCCo

Algorithm 3.2 *PaCCo*

input adjacency matrix A

$V = [\,]$; // Final Clustering

// initialize graph as one cluster
C_{init} = k-PaCCo (k = 1, A)

// cluster
V = splitCluster (C_{init}, A, V)

$k = |V|$ // number of clusters
return V

---

the adjacency matrix $A = (a_{ij})$ containing $n \times n$ entries of the form

$$a_{ij} = \begin{cases} w_{ij} & \text{, if } e_{ij} \in E \\ 0 & \text{otherwise} \end{cases}$$

with w_{ij} being the weight of edge e_{ij}. The matrix A of the undirected graph G was, therefore, square and symmetric. On-diagonal entries were defined set zero, $\text{diag}(A) = \{a_{11}, \ldots, a_{nn}\} = 0$, as we considered no self-interactions. Self-interactions of nodes did not alter the clustering result of *PaCCo* since they were – by definition – never be between two clusters.

Graph clustering was a partitioning of the graph into k disjoint clusters $C = \{C_1, \ldots, C_k\}$. A cluster C_l was a set of nodes $V_l = \{v_1, \ldots, v_m\}$ which described a corresponding subgraph $G_l = (V_l, E_l)$, with $m = |C_l|$ being the number of nodes contained in the subgraph and $|E_l|$ being the number of edges between the nodes $\{v_i, v_j\} \in V_l$. The sub-adjacency matrix A_l had the dimensionality $m \times m$.

As a result of the cluster definition, clusters were always located around the diagonal of the adjacency matrix, since a node cannot be part of two clusters at the same time. Restructuring of the adjacency matrix was always a simultaneous sorting of rows and columns.

Cluster Costs

For graph compression based on nodes we calculated the coding costs of each cluster $c(C_l)$ as a sum of the costs of each cluster node v_i, like

$$c(C_l) = \sum_{v_i \in C_l} c(v_i|C_l).$$

Nodes within one cluster shared higher similarities to one another than to nodes outside the cluster. *K-PaCCo* clustering simultaneously maximized the number of edges as well as the weight similarities inside a cluster. In other words, we clustered highly interconnected nodes with similar edge weights. Thus, the coding costs of a node v_i in a cluster C_l were determined by two factors: (1) the cluster weights of edges enclosed by C_l and (2) the number of links (edges) inside a cluster while correcting for links to other clusters. We formalized the weight and the linkage coding costs of each node within a cluster separately as

$$c(v_i|C_l) = c_{weights}(v_i|C_l) + c_{linkage}(v_i|C_l).$$

Cluster Edge Weights

A key feature of *PaCCo* was that clusters shared similar weight information. To actually code the edge weights of cluster we introduced a new concept to approximate a cluster with a weight representative. We modeled edge weight similarities to be originated from a common probability density function (PDF). Without any prior knowledge, *PaCCo* identified the underlying cluster PDF which was constantly adjusted during runtime. Thereby we accounted not only for clusters with a unique weight distribution but also for clusters without concrete weight similarity by approximat-

3.3 Improved Weighted Graph Clustering with PaCCo

ing them with large variance (practically background PDF information). A technique to compress any PDF was coding according to Huffman. The coding was defined as the inverse logarithm of an object's probability. This negative log-likelihood was exploited to calculate to coding costs $c_{weights}$ which actually coded the weights of a node v_i in the cluster C_l given a PDF:

$$c_{weights}(v_i|C_l) = -\log_2(f_{PDF}(v_i)).$$

We specified the approximation of the weights inside the subgraph of a cluster with a Gaussian distribution (GD). We chose to use a GD to get a rough approximation of the edge weights, since many natural processes already produced Gaussian data. Note, that the assumption of a Gaussian model was not a severe restriction: The GD was only part of the codebook which was mainly used to compare several candidate clustering. Thus, best model selection for data compression did not restrict the dataset to follow exactly a GD. Although optimal compression may not always achieved for non-Gaussian datasets with a Gaussian codebook, the model selection with the Gaussian codebook was nonetheless applicable for approximately symmetric data distributions. The benefit of using a GD was runtime, since its mean and standard deviation were fast computed and did not have to be estimated with any heuristic. Without prior knowledge on the underlying weight distribution – if at all specifiable – we used the GD as a suitable compromise between computational costs and accurate PDF approximations. Note, that the PDF may easily be exchanged for another PDF if the weight distribution on the edge weights is known.

Given the weighted edges in a graph interlinking the cluster nodes, the suitable cluster representative of the subgraph was introduced as a PDF $f_{GD}(w_{C_l})$ on the weights w_{C_l} of inter-cluster edges. We defined our coding costs with respect to the GD where a cluster C_l has a characteristic cluster mean μ_{C_l} and a standard deviation σ_{C_l} of all weights in one cluster. Each node in a cluster was compressed as

$$c_{weights}(v_i|C_l) = -\log_2(f_{GD}(v_i; \mu_{C_l}, \sigma_{C_l}))$$

where f_{GD} was defined for an existing edge weight w_{ij} like

$$f_{GD}(w_{ij}; \mu_{C_l}, \sigma_{C_l}) = \frac{1}{\sqrt{2\pi\sigma_{C_l}^2}} e^{-\frac{(w_{ij}-\mu_{C_l})^2}{2\sigma_{C_l}^2}}.$$

The idea was to fit a node with its set of edges into the GD by determining the edge weights with respect to all nodes v_j in the cluster:

$$f_{GD}(v_i; \mu_{C_l}, \sigma_{C_l}) = \frac{1}{|C_l|} \sum_{\forall v_j \in C_l} \frac{1}{\sqrt{2\pi\sigma_{C_l}^2}} e^{-\frac{(w_{ij}-\mu_{C_l})^2}{2\sigma_{C_l}^2}}.$$

Cluster Linkage

In addition to the weight coding costs, the inner cluster connectivity $c_{linkage}$ had to be maximized in a cluster while connections to other clusters had to be punished. If the node v_i was assigned to a cluster C_l, it caused the following linkage coding costs which were determined by the edges to nodes of the cluster $v_{j'} \in C_l$, $\forall e_{i,j'} \in E$, and the node degree ($v_{j''} \in C$, $\forall e_{i,j''} \in E$) as

$$c_{linkage}(v_i|C_l) = -.5\log_2(|e_{i,j'}|) + .5\log_2(|e_{i,j''}|).$$

We directly compressed the number of edges of a node to one cluster as well as to the other clusters, in order to balance the intra- and inter-cluster edges of clusters. Thereby, the existing number of edges of a node to a cluster was maximized, since we corrected for the number of links to the cluster C_l with the number of total edges the node v_i has.

3.3 Improved Weighted Graph Clustering with PaCCo

3.3.5 k-PaCCo Bisecting Strategy

Taking a step back from the formal definition of the cluster representatives, the *PaCCo* core routine *k-PaCCo* performed the actual clustering of any graph into k non-empty clusters. During runtime, the *k-PaCCo* routine partitioned (super-)clusters always into $k = 2$ new clusters. We integrated the objective function of model costs into the k-means strategy to cluster a graph (Algorithm 3.3). Thereby two steps were implemented as follows:

Reassignment step. The reassignment step minimized the objective function for model costs. The idea was to maximize the connectivity and similarity of each cluster, while implicitly taking care of minimizing the connectivity and similarity between the clusters. In other words, the reassignment of a node v_i to the best fitting cluster C_{new} was determined by

$$C_{new}(v_i) = \min_{C_l \in C} c(v_i | C_l)$$

Note, that we minimized the costs of a node which was equivalent to a better graph compression.

Update step. The update step explicitly adjusted weight distributions per cluster. The number of links were already precomputed during the reassignment step, thus, require no update. The update of the weight distribution in each cluster was achieved by updating the mean μ_{C_l} and standard deviation σ_{C_l} of the node costs with respect to all weights w_{ij} entirely enclosed by the cluster:

$$\mu_{C_l} = \frac{\sum w_{ij}}{n}, \quad \forall v_i, v_j \in C_l, \; v_i \neq v_j$$

Accordingly for σ_{C_l}.

The objective function (model costs of C) was always minimized or kept equal during the reassignment as well as the update step.

Algorithm 3.3 *k-PaCCo*

input k, Adjacency Matrix A, μ, σ

clustering $C = [\,]$;
assign o_i to initial cluster PDF with μ and σ

iter = iteration counter
while cluster assignment changes & iter < maxIteration **do**
  for all Objects $o_i \in A$ **do**
    reassign o_i to cluster by $c(v_i|C_l)$
  end for
  for all $C_l \in C$ **do**
    update cluster representative μ_{C_l}, σ_{C_l}
  end for
end while

3.3.6 PaCCo Splitting Strategy

PaCCo performed the splitting of a graph with the top-down approach (Algorithm 3.4). To perform the split of a (sub)graph we had the option to either randomly assign the nodes to a new cluster or direct the splitting to initial clusters better than random and subsequently save runtime. For non-random splitting the edges and their edge weights were considered. We implemented a heuristic to drive the separation of the cluster weights. Since we already had information on the GD spanning all cluster weights, the two new subclusters were initialized by shifting the GD one standard deviation up and one down on the weight distribution spectrum. Figure 3.5 depicts the subcluster initialization. In other words, the current cluster C_l to be split, might have subsumed at least two real clusters. Thus, the GD of the two subclusters was torn apart on the weight spectrum. Assuming the initial GD to subsume two clusters with separate weights, we initialized the subclustering the knowledge of the cluster to be split instead of a random initialization of the two new GD during a cluster bisection step.

3.3 Improved Weighted Graph Clustering with PaCCo

Algorithm 3.4 PaCCo's splitclusters

input Graph Partitioning C, Adjacency Matrix A, Final Clustering V

for all $C_l \in C$ **do**
  if $k < \text{size}(A_l)$ OR $1 < |C_l|$ **then**

    // Prepare two PDFs for cluster bisection
    $\mu' = [\mu_{C_l} + \sigma_{C_l}; \mu_{C_l} - \sigma_{C_l}];$
    $\sigma' = [\sigma_{C_l}/2; \sigma_{C_l}/2];$

    $C_{l_{split}} = k\text{-}PaCCo\ (k = 2, A_l; \mu', \sigma');$

    if Model-Cost$(G_{l_{split}}|C_{l_{split}}) \geq$ Model-Cost$(G_l|C_l)$ **then**
      // present cluster C_l is already good
      $V = V \cup C_l;$
    else
      // bisection of cluster "pays off"
      splitClusters$(C_{l_{split}}, A_l, V);$
    end if
  else
    $V = V \cup C_l;$
  end if
end for

return V

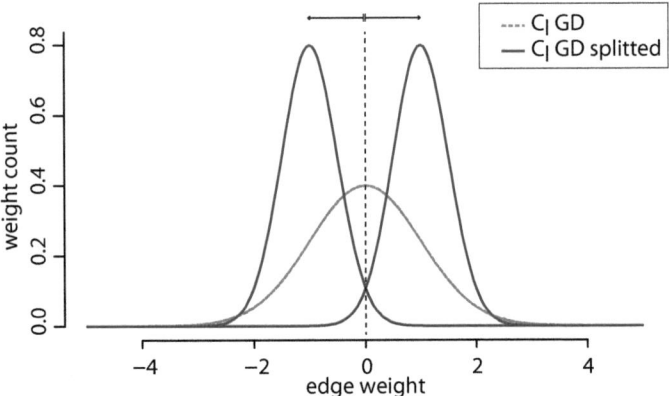

Figure 3.5: Initialization of a cluster split for k-*PaCCo* given a current cluster C_l GD (green curve). Thus, the approximation of the weights inside C_l were torn apart to obtain a guess of the possible underlying data (both red curves).

The top-down iterative splitting was performed until the coding costs of a cluster were cheaper than itself being split. As a lower convergence criterion the algorithm split the graph into singletons. To evaluate if (sub)graph splitting with Model-Cost($G_{l_{split}}|C_{l_{split}}$) resulted in a stronger compression than the (sub)graph with Model-Cost($G_l|C_l$), we split the graph only when the model costs were minimized as

$$\text{Model-Cost}(G_{l_{split}}|C_{l_{split}}) < \text{Model-Cost}(G_l|C_l).$$

Note, that the parameter costs $c(p)$ of a clustering had to be considered. In *PaCCo*, we carried along the costs for saving all μ and σ of each cluster (thus the parameter costs p directly depend on the number of clusters k). We coded both parameters with floating point precision. Since we only bisected each cluster separately, we accounted only for one additional GD to be compressed.

3.3.7 Benchmark Results of PaCCo

Although many graph clustering approaches are available today, only few were applicable to weighted graphs. In general, we selected approaches for benchmarking the performance of *PaCCo* which were not only well-known in the data mining field, but also in other communities, e.g. life science research. For detailed reviews on graph mining refer to Schaeffer (2007) and Fortunato (2010).

We conducted multiple experiments to evaluate the performance and accuracy of our novel algorithm *PaCCo*. In our extensive evaluation we compared the results of *PaCCo* to three other existing weighted graph clustering approaches. Two of the three comparative methods were parameter dependent; both algorithms required a parameter which influenced the number of clusters to be obtained. (1) We used the multilevel partitioning technique Metis (Karypis and Kumar 1998a) which required the number of clusters k as parameter. (2) The MCL (Stijn 2000) required an inflation parameter which directly influenced the granularity of the clustering, thus, the number of clusters. In addition, one of the three comparative methods was parameter-free. (3) The spectral clustering approach by Zelnik-Manor and Perona (2004) was a parameter-free variant of spectral clustering algorithms (in the following named SpectralZM).

With regard to the parameter dependent methods, we sampled the free parameter for each experiment separately and always used the best performing result for benchmarking. All experiments were performed on a 2.9 GHz Windows computer with 3 GB RAM. *PaCCo* was implemented in Java.

We generated several synthetic weighted graphs varying the number of noise edges added to the weighted graphs, the spacing between the means of the cluster distributions, and the number of clusters k. Since we generated the graph cluster by cluster, we had information on the class label of each node which we used for benchmarking of the algorithms. As real world example we used the weighted undirected protein network of a protein interaction screen by Costanzo et al. (2010), which was evaluated using the modularity measure as no class labels were present. In addition, we evaluated the clustering result with respect to biological enrichment.

Synthetic Data Description

PaCCo was designed to compress the graph weights with a GD. To demonstrate that other weight distributions were compressed equally well, we used three underlying distributions. These underlying distributions for the edge weights in the synthetic graphs were either Gaussian, uniform, or Laplacian. As a result each experiment was executed three times, once using Gaussian distributions, once with uniformly distributed cluster distributions, and once using Laplacian distributions. The default number of nodes per cluster for all synthetic experiments was set to 50. Each cluster of 50 nodes was randomly interlinked with 70 % intra-cluster edges. After a synthetic graph was generated the nodes were randomly shuffled to enhance complexity in the clustering process. If not specified elsewhere, we generated $k = 20$ clusters, which corresponded to a total amount of 1,000 nodes and around 17,000 edges in the weighted graph.

For Metis and MCL we selected the parameters as follows: The number of clusters required for Metis was given in all synthetic datasets, thus was directly set k to the given value; the inflation parameter required for MCL was set to the default value of 1.4 for all synthetic experiments as this parameter also achieved the best results.

For evaluating the clustering performance a simple calculation of precision or accuracy was not possible for graph clustering, since the cluster identities were interchangeable. Therefore, we computed equivalent measures based on information theoretic measures, which was applicable due to the fact that class labels were present for the synthetic data. We decided to choose the best of the four measures presented in Vinh et al. (2009) for clus-

3.3 Improved Weighted Graph Clustering with PaCCo

tering comparison, namely the adjusted mutual information (AMI). AMI measured the agreement between two clustering results based on entropy. AMI had a fixed value range allowing a direct comparison of different approaches, which scaled between 0 and 1 for a random or a perfect clustering result, respectively. AMI value of 1 and 0 correspond to a perfect cluster agreement and a clustering agreement expected by chance, respectively. In contrast to the normalized mutual information (Strehl and Ghosh 2003), AMI was corrected for chance.

Synthetic Noise Edges

First, we evaluated how well the graph clustering algorithms handled additional edges in the graph, which we call noise edges. In addition to the approximately 17,000 intra-cluster edges, the number of noise edges, which were additional edges randomly added to random nodes, present in the data was varied from 0 to 20,000 (roughy 0–118 %). The noise in the data was represented by inter-cluster edges being added to the data, thus, introducing inter-cluster connectivity to hamper cluster separation. The number of clusters was kept constant at $k = 20$, the means of all cluster distributions were separated by 1, and the standard deviation of all cluster distributions was chosen to be 1.

The more edge noise we added to the graph, all four approaches resulted in a decrease of their clustering performance, as measured by the information theoretic measure AMI (Figure 3.6). MCL was only able to handle data with up to 10,000 (roughly 60 %) inter-cluster edges independent of the underlying distributions. As soon as noise was added the performance started to decrease. SpectralZM had large performance fluctuations while processing the noise data for all three data distributions. Even in the dataset containing no noise it was not able to achieve an optimal clustering. Metis performed slightly worse on the Laplacian dataset than on the Gaussian and uniform data, having a constant decrease with increased noise. *PaCCo* was

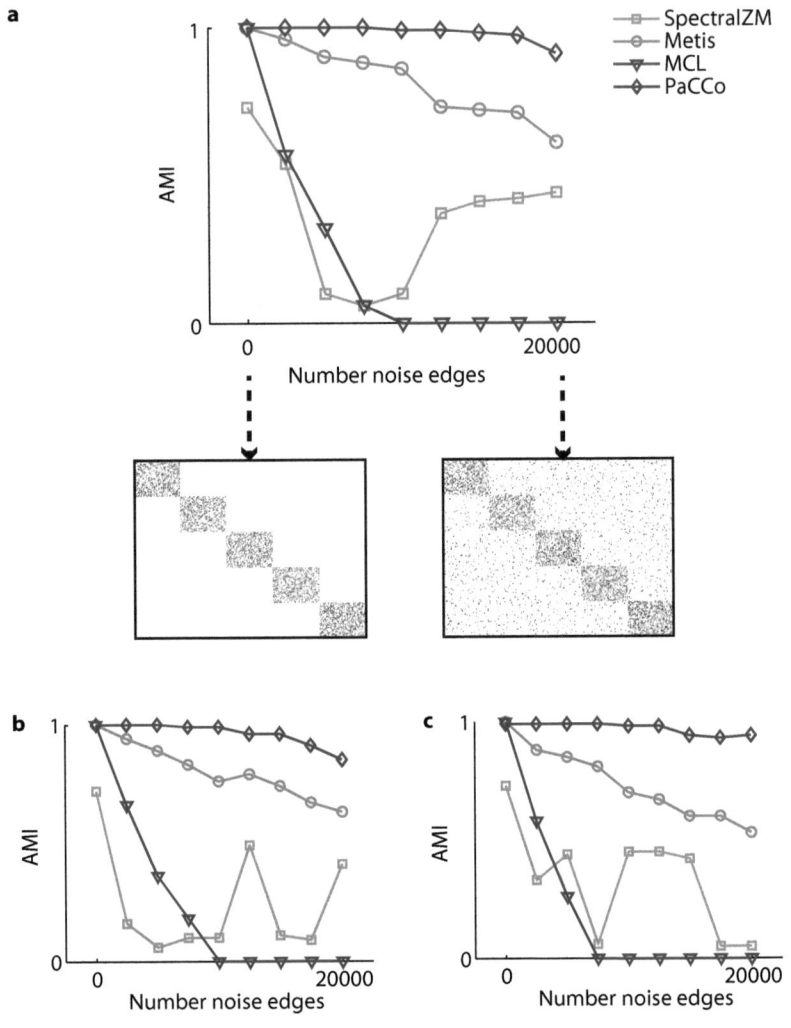

Figure 3.6: Varying the number of inter-cluster edges (noise edges). The number of noise edges were added to the graph in addition to the existing edges. The weighted graph has 1,000 nodes ($k=20$ clusters with each 50 nodes) and has (without noise) 70 % of intra-cluster edges (17,000 intra-cluster edges). Means and standard deviation of the cluster distributions were set to 1. Adjacency matrices in **a.** exemplify the range of graph used for experiments. Underlying cluster distributions were **a.** Gaussian, **b.** uniform, and **c.** Laplacian.

3.3 Improved Weighted Graph Clustering with PaCCo

the only algorithm which was able to achieve better results than the other three methods for increased noise; even for the largest number of noise edges *PaCCo* outperformed the other three graph clustering methods.

Synthetic Variation of Weight Distribution

Second, cluster weights' intervals were varied, having a constant cluster value of $k = 20$ with additional 5,000 inter-cluster edges. Starting with all 20 means of the cluster distributions around a mean of 1, they were gradually spread out until the means of the cluster distributions were separated by 1; As a result the lowest cluster distribution mean was 1 and the highest cluster distribution mean was 20. Thus, we altered the numerical spaces between the cluster weights.

How did the algorithms respond to a change of the cluster weights (Figure 3.7)? MCL and SpectralZM performed poorly with AMI indices between 0 and 0.5. Metis increased performance when the cluster weights were clearly separated than with all weights being equal for each cluster for the Gaussian and the uniform distributed data. On the Laplacian dataset Metis also achieved overall poor results like MCL and SpectralZM. Gradually changing the spacing of the cluster weights means, *PaCCo* achieved the best overall results for all three cluster distributions showing the highest benefit for the Laplacian dataset. This result demonstrated that *PaCCo* was able to perform better on weighted graphs than all other approaches independent on the underlying data distribution.

Synthetic Dataset Sizes

Finally, the number of clusters k was varied from 10 to 100, each containing 50 nodes, leading to a maximum of 5,000 nodes, while approximately 70 % of the intra-cluster edges (roughly 9,000 to 90,000 intra-cluster edges) were connected and 30 % of these intra-cluster edges were added as inter-cluster

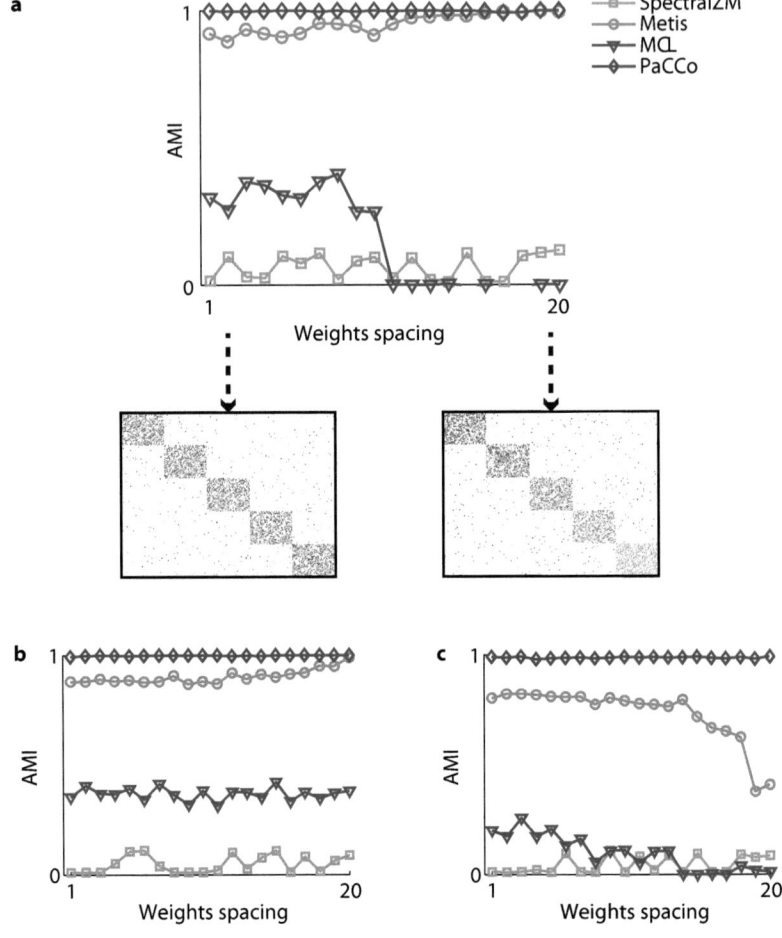

Figure 3.7: Varying the cluster weights' spacing intervals. The underlying cluster distributions were **a.** Gaussian, **b.** uniform, and **c.** Laplacian. The number of clusters was set to $k = 20$ with 70 % of intra-cluster edges (approximately 17,000 intra-cluster edges) being connected, and ca. 5,000 inter-cluster edges considered as noise being present in the data. One on the x-axis indicated that all means of the cluster distributions had a value of one, while 20 on the x-axis indicated that cluster distribution means were all different being separated by one unit each. Therefore, the lowest cluster distribution mean was 1 and the largest cluster distribution mean had a value of 20. Adjacency matrices in **a.** exemplify the range of graph used for experiments. Underlying cluster distributions were **a.** Gaussian, **b.** uniform, and **c.** Laplacian.

3.3 Improved Weighted Graph Clustering with PaCCo

edges (i.e. ca. 3,000 to 30,000 inter-cluster edges). The mean and standard deviation of all cluster distributions were set to 1.

Varying the number of clusters k (Figure 3.8) should be a trivial task for each algorithm. Metis achieved convincing results for the Gaussian and the uniform distributed cluster distributions but showed no satisfactory results for the Laplacian dataset. MCL was only able to perform well for larger datasets with uniformly distributed data. In all other cases it obtained poor results. SpectralZM was not able to achieve convincing results in any of the given datasets. In contrast to all other methods, our parameter-free approach *PaCCo* achieved equally good results, independent of the number of clusters for the Gaussian, the uniform, and the Laplacian distributed data. Note, that this version of *PaCCo* can only handle datasets which can be fully loaded as matrix into the virtual memory similar to SpectralZM.

Runtime

For runtime comparisons we varied again the number of clusters k from 10 to 100, while each cluster contained 50 nodes. Approximately 70 % of the intra cluster edges were connected and no inter-cluster edges were present. The mean and standard deviation of all cluster distributions were set to 1. In order to obtain accurate runtime results each dataset was processed 10 times by each method, subsequently averaging ten rounds.

The runtime of one execution of each algorithm was recorded. Importantly, for the parameter dependent methods Metis and MCL we first had to sample for optimal parameter setting before actually tracking the execution time of one run. We did not account for this time effort here. Due to the fact that, to our knowledge, the approach by Zelnik-Manor and Perona (2004) was the only existing weighted graph clustering algorithm without requiring parameters equal to our approach, thus the runtimes of SpectralZM and *PaCCo* were directly comparable.

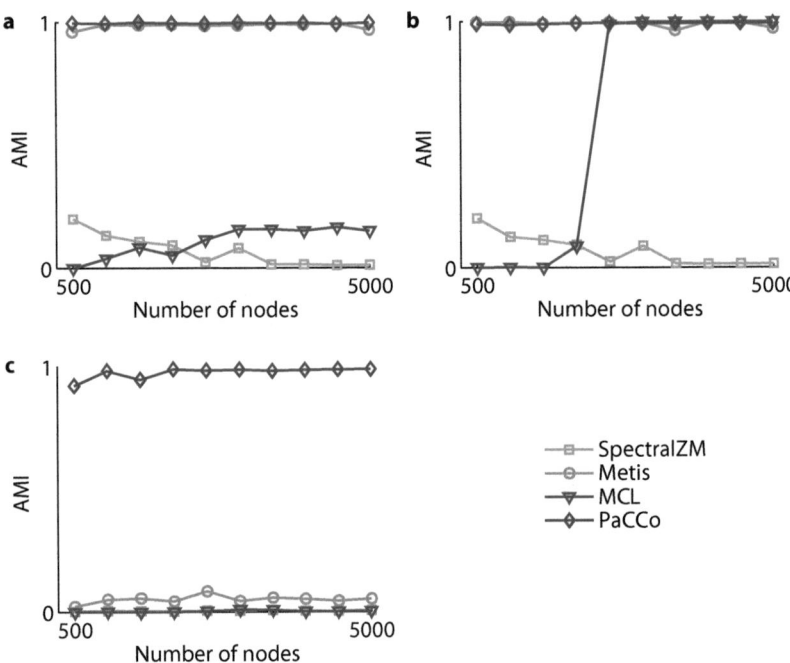

Figure 3.8: Varying the number of clusters k from 10 to 100, each containing 50 nodes. The underlying cluster distributions were **a.** Gaussian, **b.** uniform, and **c.** Laplacian. Approximately 70 % of the intra-cluster edges were connected (i.e. ca. 9,000 to 90,000 intra-cluster edges) and additionally 30 % of these intra-cluster edges were added as inter-cluster edges being considered as noise (i.e. ca. 3,000 to 30,000 inter-cluster edges). The mean and standard deviation of all cluster distributions was set to a value of 1.

3.3 Improved Weighted Graph Clustering with PaCCo

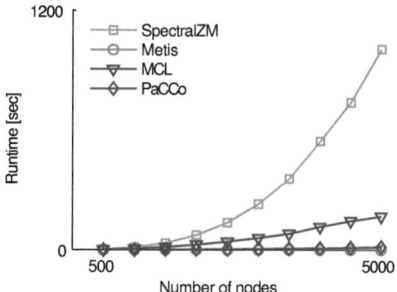

Figure 3.9: Runtime for graphs of increasing size. The runtime of the parameter-free methods *PaCCo* and Spectral, as well as the runtime of Metis and MCL.

The runtime of *PaCCo* and SpectralZM (Figure 3.9) clearly showed that *PaCCo* was faster than SpectralZM. While SpectralZM had a time complexity of $O(n^3)$ due to the eigenvalue decomposition, *PaCCo*'s time complexity was only super-linear. For example, having 5,000 nodes in a graph SpectralZM required 16.8 minutes to obtain a clustering result while *PaCCo* only 14.1 seconds. Thus, *PaCCo* was approximately 70 times faster than SpectralZM. *PaCCo* was even faster than the parameter dependent approach MCL, while being slightly slower than Metis.

Interactome Real-world Dataset

We evaluated the clustering result of *PaCCo* on the above defined yeast synthetic lethal *interactome* real dataset generated by high-throughput biology. Clustering performance on PPI should not only be evaluated on the number of enriched modules but also on how well graph structures are uncovered (Song and Singh 2009). We used modularity as evaluation function of the cluster strength, since no class label information was available for the nodes. Modularity was widely used as quality and objective function

(Danon et al. 2005, Fortunato 2010, Girvan and Newman 2002). As already defined, weighted definition of modularity was used for evaluation.

Biologists were able to determine whether two genes of an organism are genetically interacting. In that sense, the deletion of one gene from the organism had no effect on the fitness of an organism, but the deletion of an additional gene resulted in a significant fitness defect. The so called double knockout may be either lethal to the organism (called synthetic lethal), or in contrast resulted in increased fitness, thus, stronger growth. Note, that two proteins which were synthetic lethal supposably acted in two parallel pathways, where one can compensated for the loss of the other. In the synthetic lethal screen (Costanzo et al. 2010), two yeast genes were simultaneously deleted while the increased (positive) or decreased (negative) colony growth is read out and used as edge weight in the PPI.

We applied *PaCCo* and SpectralZM without parameter setting while Metis and MCL were sampled for k and inflation. Figure 3.10 depicts the graph clustering details for the best run of each algorithm. Metis performed best for $k = 3$ and MCL for the default inflation parameter of 1.4 (resulting in $k=1121$) when evaluated for clustering modularity. *PaCCo* and SpectralZM automatically identified 11 and 3 clusters. The number of clusters found by SpectralZM and MCL were extreme: SpectralZM generated 3 clusters whereas MCL generated only singleton clusters except for one. *PaCCo* identified 11 clusters of the yeast synthetic *interactome* with the best clustering structure (Figure 3.11) – even better than the SA clustering which in turn failed to generate globally best solution. The bisecting strategy of *PaCCo* was able to cope with the unusually high connectivity and with the edge distribution of positive and negative edges.

Clusters of the synthetic lethal *interactome* interaction network were biologically evaluated with the help of the gene ontology (GO) database (Ashburner et al. 2000). GO contained functional annotations of proteins, which we used to calculate statistical enrichment of GO molecular

3.3 Improved Weighted Graph Clustering with PaCCo

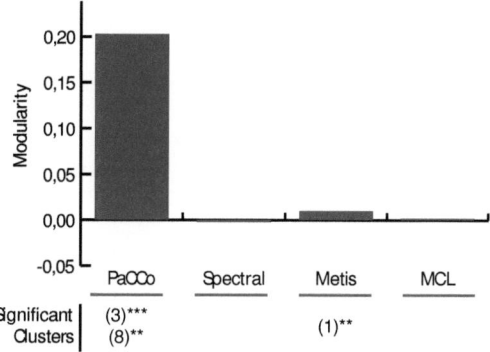

Figure 3.10: Performance on synthetic lethal *interactome* dataset. The best clustering result of each algorithm shown as a bar graph. We measured performance by modularity. In addition, if the best clustering also enriched a molecular function, we denoted the number of the cluster e.g. (3) with its significance level ($**p < .05$, $***p < .01$).

functions (Figure 3.10). With the hypergeometric probability, statistically significant functions for each non-singleton cluster were identified according to Brohee et al. (2008). Only with *PaCCo* the graph clustering result was enriched for two molecular functions, whereby, Metis was enriched for one of the two enrichments found by *PaCCo* . SpectralZM and MCL clustering did not generate any significant results. *PaCCo* and Metis were both enriched for *hydrolase activity*, suggesting that synthetic lethality was more likely to be part of two parallel functional pathways. Proteins of the hydrolase activity class catalyzed an essential chemical reaction called hydrolysis during which water molecules were split. The *PaCCo* clustering was able to enrich for *hydrolase activity* even better than Metis (Figure 3.10, *PaCCo* cluster no. 3 and Metis cluster no. 1). Interestingly, *PaCCo* was able to reveal another cluster enriched for *isomerase activity*, not identified by any other algorithm. Isomerase proteins took care of structural arrangements of isomers. Isomers were proteins which were structurally different while their molecular formula stayed constant. This essential process may even inhibit or enable proper protein function.

Shared Features in Weighted Graphs

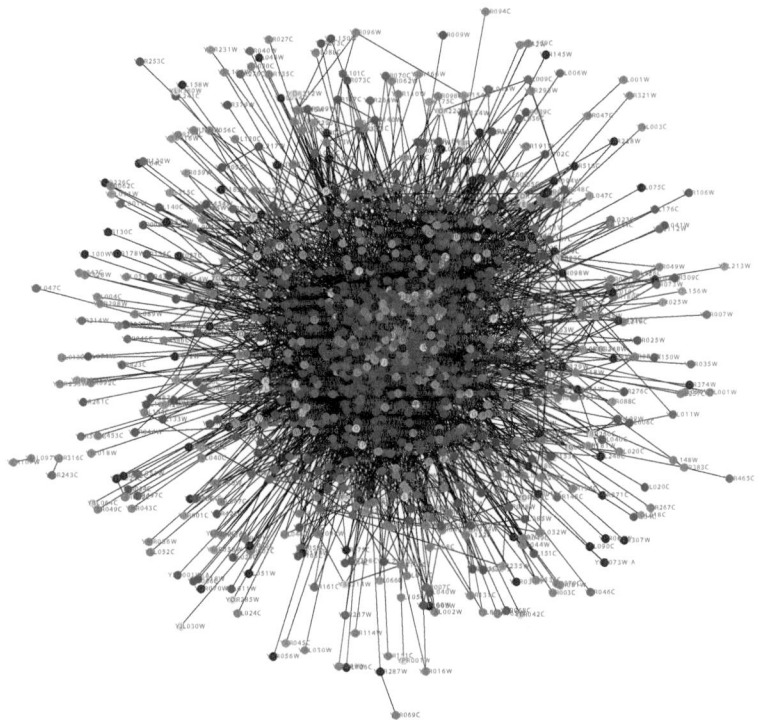

Figure 3.11: Yeast Synthetic Lethal *Interactome*. Clustered with *PaCCo*, nodes were colored in 11 different colors to indicate cluster membership of nodes.

Benchmark Conclusion

Our result allowed to conclude that the parameter-free algorithm *PaCCo* was demonstrated to outperform the other methods. MCL was not able to handle noise and, in addition, requires the setting of an inflation parameter. Metis was not able to handle increasing noise and additionally required the number of clusters in the data which for real data was rarely known. SpectralZM showed difficulties with respect to noise present in the graphs as well as with respect to graph size.

For the experimental data *PaCCo* was able to find a strong clustering result regarding the modularity measure, in contrast to all other approaches which did not succeed in yielding comparable results. Moreover, *PaCCo* outperformed the other algorithms with regard to biologically meaningful clusters.

The experiments demonstrated that *PaCCo* outperformed the three methods in most settings while being faster than parameter-free SpectralZM and comparable to the parameter dependent methods Metis and MCL.

3.4 Conclusion and Outlook

We proposed *PaCCo* – a parameter-free clustering for weighted graphs. *PaCCo* successfully coupled a bisecting k-means strategy with a graph compression principle which turned out be an efficient and accurate graph clustering technique. Since *PaCCo* was parameter-free and fully automatic as well as subsequently easily applicable to real weighted graphs without requiring any parameters like the number of subgroups present in the data or available evaluation criteria. Moreover, our clustering results did not suffer from long runtime. When compared to the initial SA heuristic to find globally optimal clustering, *PaCCo* was able to better cope with highly connected graphs, in order to yield significant results. *PaCCo* supported the analysis of weighted graphs, such as PPI networks, by revealing interesting and relevant clusters.

To further improve *PaCCo* weighted graph clustering, several aspects may be addressed. Graphs were only clustered when the corresponding adjacency matrix was fully loaded into the virtual memory. Using indexing strategies or a simple edge list will allow clustering of larger graphs. Furthermore, graph compression is in general only a summing up of individual building blocks within the object function. For example, edges to a cluster were independent of the similarity to the weights in the model costs. As a consequence nodes may be assigned to a cluster based on their edge similarity and not high linkage. Calculation of the objective function (model costs) may mathematically couple the ideas by only evaluating edge weight similarity when linkage to a cluster is high enough, instead of sole summing up of individual costs. Finally, the hard bisection of the graph may be converted to a "soft bisection". Therein the bisecting step will only be used to open up a new cluster but allow nodes of the entire graph to be reassigned instead of node subsets. Implementations of all aspects should, however, always be considered with respect to overall runtime of *PaCCo*.

4 Differential Dependencies

To understand the molecular level of many human diseases, such as cancer, lipid quantifications have been shown to offer an excellent opportunity to reveal disease-specific regulations. The data analysis of a cell's *lipidome*, however, remains a challenging task and cannot be accomplished solely based on intuitive reasoning. We have developed a method to identify a lipid correlation network which was entirely disease-specific. A powerful method to correlate experimentally measured lipid levels across various samples was a Gaussian Graphical Model (GGM), which is based on partial correlation coefficients. In contrast to regular Pearson correlations, partial correlations aim to identify only direct correlations while eliminating indirect associations. Conventional GGM calculations on the entire dataset did, however, not provide information on whether a correlation was truly disease-specific with respect to the disease samples and not a correlation of control samples. Thus, we implemented a novel differential GGM (dGGM) approach unraveling only the disease-specific correlations, and applied it to the *lipidome* of immortal Glioblastoma tumor cells. A large set of lipid species was measured by mass spectrometry (MS) in order to evaluate lipid remodeling as a result to a combination of perturbation of cells inducing programmed cell death, while the other perturbations served solely as biological controls. With the dGGM, we were able to reveal Glioblastoma-specific lipid correlations to advance biomedical research on novel gene therapies.

The part of this chapter on dGGM was published in collaboration with the groups of Anke Meyer-Bäse and Fabian Theis in Müller et al. (2011b).

4.1 Biological Question and Data

4.1.1 Lipidomes

The *lipidome* is the set of all lipids in a cell and is the largest subset of the organisms metabolome. With improved methodologies, an organism's *lipidome* was resolvable. Their study is named *lipidomics* and is an emerging field offering a new level of complexity to the cells molecular resolution. The *lipidome* has optimal properties to be analyzed by MS (Harkewicz and Dennis 2010). Recently, the yeast *lipidome* was quantified by high-throughput MS yielding roughly 250 lipids across 21 lipid classes (Ejsing et al. 2009) while the *lipidome* of mammalian cells was estimated to comprise hundreds of thousands of lipids (Harkewicz and Dennis 2010). The lipids are mainly organized in membranes encompassing each cell or cell organelles. Building the membranes together with proteins, lipids play a large role in cell signaling. As a result lipids became more and more relevant to all kinds of diseases. With MS the role lipids play in diseases, such as cancer, became accessible for organism-wide screening.

Lipids were grouped into lipid classes based on their chemical properties. Single lipid classes were differentiated by their lipid head groups while the linked fatty acids may vary. For the human system, several pathways described the remodeling steps of the head groups alone (Figure 4.1, derived from KEGG Kanehisa et al. (2010)). Extracts of the following three pathways were merged to form the head group remodeling pathways rele-

4.1 Biological Question and Data

vant to the analyzed lipids: Glycerophospholipid metabolism, sphingolipid metabolism and ganglio series of glycosphingolipid metabolism.

4.1.2 Lipidome Correlations

When comparing measurements of components in a diseased and control state, the standard approach was to analyze their differential "expression" or abundance. Whenever a comparison between two or more sample types was not applicable, correlation analyses were usually applied to identify two components with comparable response patterns. However, correlation analyses with respect to their differential nature has yet not been addressed.

4.1.3 The Human Glioblastoma Lipidome

The *in vitro* model of human Glioblastoma brain tumors is the U87 cell line. Recent studies showed that the combined perturbation of gene transfection with the p53 tumor suppressor gene prior to chemotherapy with SN-38 triggered cell death (modest apoptosis and cell cycle arrest in G2) in the otherwise immortal Glioblastoma cell line (He et al. 2010, Puchades et al. 2007). Note that the U87 GM cell lines carry the wt p53 tumor suppressor gene, and not a mutant version. SN-38 is a topoisomerase-I inhibitor inducing DNA damage, like DNA double strand breaks (Voigt et al. 1998) and decreased the level of Galectin-I in U87 cells.

Lipidome Quantification

To analyze the lipid variations as a response to the effective perturbation, high-throughput MS experiments were conducted as follows: U87 were lysed after perturbation and subsequently quantified with MS yielding the lipid quantification (Figure 4.2). In detail, cell lysates of all perturbed cell lines were analyzed for variations of lipid levels (Bing et al. 2007, He et al.

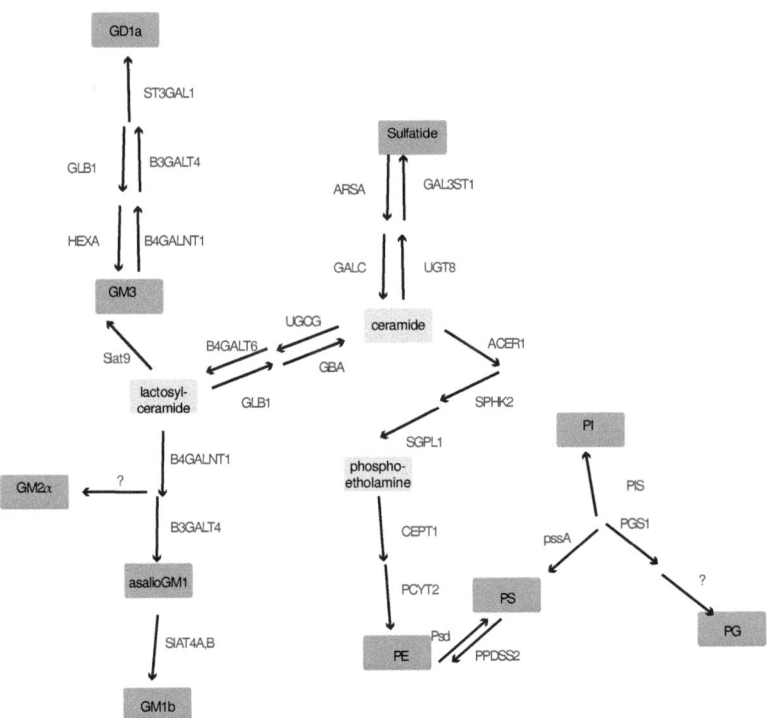

Figure 4.1: Lipid Head Group Remodeling Pathway. Excerpt of the metabolism of the lipid classes covered by the *lipidome* study. Enzymes catalyzing compound remodeling steps label the edges.

4.1 Biological Question and Data

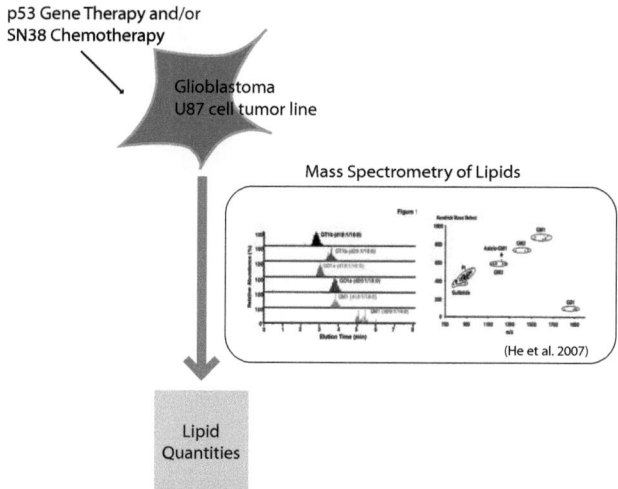

Figure 4.2: From Cells to Lipid Correlations. U87 cell lines were perturbed and subsequently lysed prior to MS analysis. Lipid classes were separable by their mass over charge and mass defect. Subsequently, lipid concentrations of 167 polar lipid species were obtained.

2010) with a specialized Fourier-Transform Ion-Cyclotron-Resonance (FT-ICR) MS technique (Bing et al. 2007). With the FT-ICR MS, polar lipids, such as phospholipids, as well as complex glycolipids, such as gangliosides were reliably separated and identified. Intensity values of all those complex lipids were measured resulting in quantifications of each lipid across six lipid classes. As a result, quantitative measurements of relative abundance profiles of polar lipids were obtained from cell lysates, whereby lipid levels were measured.

Sample Specifications

U87 cells transfected with wt tumor suppressor gene p53 prior to treatment with the chemotherapeutic drug SN-38 underwent modest apoptosis and cell cycle arrest in G2, while chemotherapy alone did not trigger the same

Table 4.1: U87 Perturbations. List of all samples with each a different perturbation of the U87 cell line (wt). The bold faced sample was the effective perturbation of Glioblastoma cells inducing apoptosis.

Name	Perturbation
Sample 1	DI312/24hr + SN-38/24hr
Sample 2	**p53/24hr + SN-38/24hr**
Sample 3	SN-38/24hr + DI312/24hr
Sample 4	SN-38/24hr + p53/24hr
Sample 5	DI312
Sample 6	p53/24hr
Sample 7	SN-38/24hr
Control Sample	wt

phenotype (Puchades et al. 2007). The reverse order of SN-38 treatment prior to p53 transfection resulted in almost complete apoptosis and complete G2 arrest.

For reliable biological interpretation of the effective perturbation, several control perturbations were conducted. Table 4.1 lists the samples used for the study comprised of seven different perturbations and one wt control sample. DI312 was the empty adenovirus used to transfect U87 cells with the p53 gene. Thus, p53 was DI312 vector with the integrated p53 gene. Transfection and SN-38 chemotherapy was each applied over 24 hours prior to analysis. With two technical replicates of seven plus one wt sample, the *lipidome* dataset used for this study contained 167 lipid measurements of 16 MS runs.

Lipid Head Group Ambiguity

Out of the large set of the *lipidome*, 167 polar lipids were measured with FT-ICR MS across six lipid classes (varying primarily in their respective head groups). While lipid head groups were uniquely identified with MS, the associated fatty acid side chains can technically not independently resolved.

An example for a complex lipid with ambiguous fatty acid side chains was PS(C36:4) that could have e.g. C18:2/C18:2 fatty acids incorporated, but also C16:0/C20:4 or C16:2/C20:2, etc.. Note, that some lipid classes, like gangliosides, have one variable and one fixed fatty acid side chain, thus, both side chains were unambiguously inferred. The MS result – the matrix to be analyzed in this study – holds concentrations of lipids for each cell line for all perturbations.

4.2 Conventional Correlation Networks

Conventional approaches to deduce co-response patterns were performing correlation-based analyses directly generating networks. Basically, for each component measured in the present dataset, pairwise all-against-all correlation coefficients were calculated. The straight-forward method, to investigate co-response patterns were Pearson correlations with additional statistical testing of edge significance. Other derivatives of the Pearson correlation networks also included e.g. the calculation of mutual information of the coefficients (Butte et al. 2000). Only few studies published on (Pearson) correlation-networks were in the field of *lipidomics* Thus, the following correlation-based network computation with a Gaussian Graphical Model was already an adaption of statistical methods to *lipidomics*.

A method to derive conditional independence of response patterns was a GGM using the principle of partial correlation coefficients. Several studies applied partial correlation analysis mostly to *transcriptome* datasets (Magwene and Kim 2004, Schäfer and Strimmer 2005a). For the standard GGM estimation as described in the methods section analysis, the number of samples must exceed the number of variables. If, however, the number of samples is smaller, alternative approaches are to be implemented in order to estimate the GGM.

4.2.1 Gaussian Graphical Model

Figure 4.3 depicts the overall calculation flow of a GGM. In case of the present *lipidome* dataset, a correlation coefficient provided information on the degree of dependence between all measured variables. This pairwise correlation was calculated based on the measurements across all samples – the cell lines with various perturbation. Partial correlations had to be evaluated for statistical significance to ensure that the correlation did not occur by chance. Significant lipid-to-lipid correlations were gathered in the resulting GGM – an undirected weighted graph.

Traditionally, correlation networks have been used to obtain information on co-regulations of variables $L = (l_1, \ldots, l_p)$, $|L| = p$ measured across all samples $S = (s_1, \ldots, s_n)$, $|S| = n$; with $X = (x_{ls})$ the raw data matrix used for calculations.

The standard measure of pairwise correlations were Pearson product-moment correlation coefficients $P = (\rho_{ij})$, which quantify the linear dependency between two variables l_i and l_j. A common problem of Pearson correlation coefficients were indirect effects giving rise to a large variety of unspecific, but high correlation coefficients throughout -*omics* datasets (Krumsiek et al. 2011). GGMs attempted to estimate conditional dependencies between measured variables over all samples rather than marginal dependencies, thereby eliminating such indirect correlations. The derivation of partial correlation coefficients may also be explained by linear regression: The partial correlation between the lipids l_1 and l_2 was the correlation of the residuals that result from linearly regressing l_1 and l_2 against the remaining lipids $(l_3, \ldots, l_p)$. In our study, the partial correlation ζ_{ij} provided information on the co-response of two lipids l_i and l_j.

To generate a GGM, the number of samples with respect to the number of variables determined the approach used for the calculation. If the number of samples n exceeded the number of variables p, full-order partial correlations $Z = (\zeta_{ij})$ were calculated in a straight-forward manner from

4.2 Conventional Correlation Networks

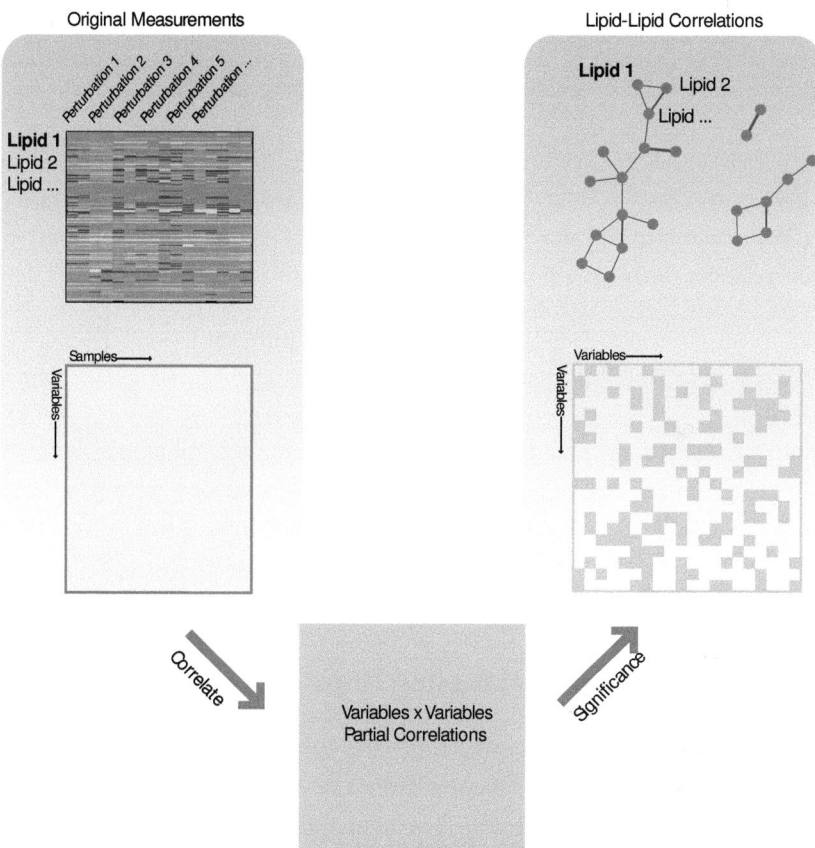

Figure 4.3: Raw Lipidome Transformed to the GGM Network. How the raw dataset of lipid measurements across various perturbations is generally transformed into lipid-lipid correlation-based network, is depicted in individual steps. The *lipidome* raw dataset was a matrix of samples over variables holding lipid quantifications for various perturbations (the samples). Pairwise correlations of lipids resulted in an undirected graph of lipid-to-lipid interactions holding the partial correlation values. Only statistically significant correlations were included in the resulting network. Edge widths indicated correlation strengths.

the inverse of the covariance matrix P as

$$\Omega = (\omega_{ij}) = P^{-1}$$

$$Z = (\zeta_{ij}) = -\omega_{ij}/\sqrt{\omega_{ii}\omega_{jj}}.$$

Statistical tests were next applied to determine whether a partial correlation ζ_{ij} was significantly different from zero ζ_{ij}^* (we mark a significant partial correlation with an asterisk) resulting in the GGM Z^*. Of the partial correlation matrix Z we constructed Z^* as

$$Z^* = (\zeta_{ij}^*) = \begin{cases} \zeta_{ij} & \text{, if } \zeta_{ij} \text{ is significant} \\ 0 & \text{, otherwise} \end{cases}$$

and we denoted $\exists \zeta_{ij}^*$ for $\zeta_{ij}^* > 0$. A GGM is an undirected graph obtained by partial correlation calculation with subsequent statistical testing for edge significance. The graph nodes represent the measured variables whereas the edge weights corresponded to significant partial correlation coefficients.

4.2.2 Regularized Gaussian Graphical Models

If the number of samples is smaller than the number of variables ($n < p$), the straight-forward GGM calculation cannot be applied but a regularization and a likelihood estimation step have to be included. For $n < p$ the covariance matrix is rank-deficient (Monakov 1994, Opgen-Rhein and Strimmer 2006, Schäfer and Strimmer 2005b), as a consequence the covariance matrix is not positive definite and can, thus, not be inverted. As a result the sample covariance is only a very poor approximation of the true covariance.

In the case of the present lipidomics data, we indeed had the case of $n < p$ with $p = 157$ lipids and $n = 8$ samples. Note, that eight samples were measured with two technical replicates and analyses were performed on the raw data including the replicates. To estimate the GGM for $n < p$,

4.2 Conventional Correlation Networks

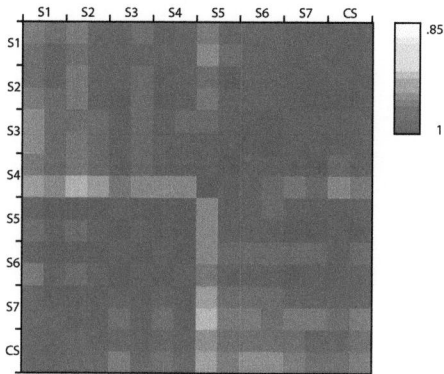

Figure 4.4: Glioblastoma GGM Correlation Network. Pairwise correlation coefficients were color-coded for comparisons of the lipid quantities of samples 1-7 (S1-7) and the control sample (CS).

Strimmer and colleagues introduced an all-in-one approach (Opgen-Rhein and Strimmer 2007, Schäfer and Strimmer 2005b). One estimation step was a shrinkage approach and was applied to obtain the true correlation matrix $\hat{P}$. The other estimation step distinguished actually existing edges from "null" edges in the GGM by fitting a statistical model assuming these two population of edges. The GGM was finally build by adjusting for local false-discovery rates (FDR) (Opgen-Rhein and Strimmer 2007, Schäfer and Strimmer 2005b). This method of regularized GGMs was already applied to transcriptomics datasets (de la Fuente et al. 2004, Magwene and Kim 2004, Schäfer and Strimmer 2005a)

4.2.3 Lipidome GGM Results

When calculating the GGM, all samples are assumed to be independent (Opgen-Rhein and Strimmer 2006), but inspection of the present *lipidome* dataset showed a strong correlation between all samples (Figure 4.4). Although correlations between the technical replicates were higher than be-

Differential Dependencies

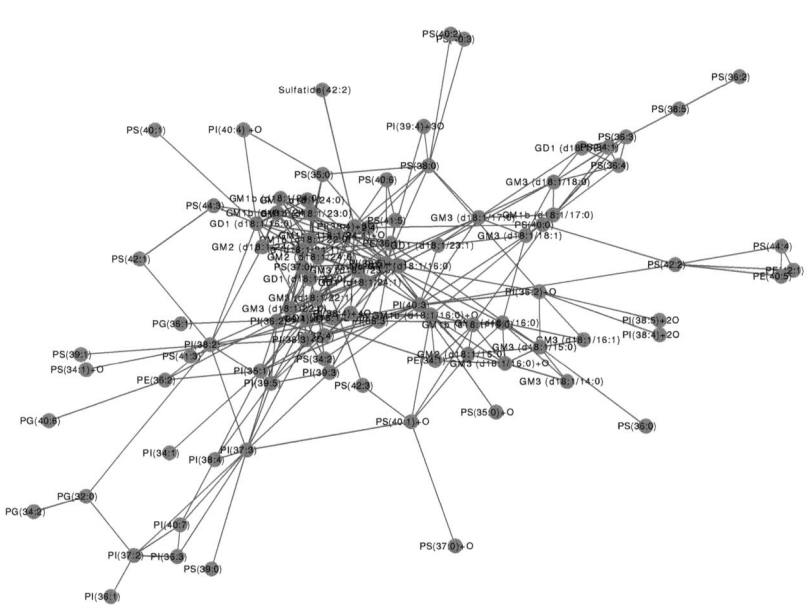

Figure 4.5: Glioblastoma GGM Correlation Network. GGM of the Glioblastoma *lipidome* measured on several perturbations. Nodes are links connected with an edge if their partial correlation was significant.

tween perturbations, the overall correlation of disease and control samples was very high (> .95). In case of dependent samples the covariance estimates were no longer optimal: its standard deviation monotonically increased with larger correlation coefficients of samples (Monakov 1994). Note that the result of the strong correlation between all samples already indicated that the successful perturbation of cells transfected with wt p53 prior to SN-38 chemotherapy had strong effects only on few lipids and not the lipid levels in general. To account for the high dependencies between samples, we calculated the GGM mimicking that all samples were replicates of one another. Since seven of the eight samples were only measured as controls (which were introduced as control replicates with respect to the one perturbation of interest), this approach was reasonable for our study.

The *lipidome* of the U87 Glioblastoma cells across all seven perturbations and wt was analyzed with a GGM (Opgen-Rhein and Strimmer 2007). Since the samples (2 technical replicates of 8 samples) exceeded the number of variables (167 lipids) in the *lipidome* dataset, a regularized GGM was used to estimate the significant partial correlations (Opgen-Rhein and Strimmer 2007). Figure 4.5 depicts the obtained GGM of the Glioblastoma *lipidome*.

4.3 Differential Gaussian Graphical Model

4.3.1 Motivation

Despite recent progress in therapy and surgical intervention, Glioblastoma multiforms, malignant primary brain tumors, are nearly always fatal. The *in vitro* model of human Glioblastoma brain tumors is the U87 cell line, the major characteristic of which is its resistance to apoptosis (programmed cell death). Recent studies showed that the combined perturbation of gene transfection with the p53 tumor suppressor gene prior to chemotherapy with SN-38 triggers cell death in the (otherwise immortal) Glioblastoma cell line (He et al. 2010, Puchades et al. 2007). At first a proteomic study showed a down-regulation of Galectin-1 in response to the combined perturbation (Puchades et al. 2007), which motivated the elucidation of lipid regulations (He et al. 2010). On an organism-wide scale, changes in complex polar lipid levels were reliably identified by a specialized MS technique (Bing et al. 2007). The set of all commonly regulated lipids will allow to reveal dysregulations of e.g. metabolic pathways or functionally similar proteins. However, the molecular details of the perturbation-affected lipid coregulations still remained to be elucidated.

In order to unravel the lipid remodeling that effected or was affected by apoptosis of U87 cells, the comparison of wt cell lines with the p53 plus SN-38 perturbations was not sufficient. For example, lipid remodeling may be the result of singular effects, like the transfection of the empty adenovirus, only the wt p53 adenovirus or solely the SN-38 chemotherapy. Only the entire dataset with all perturbations and wt allowed to statistically exploit the wealth of all perturbation effects, which were not revealed by solely comparing only two biologically relevant perturbations.

We aimed to identify partial correlations of lipid concentrations while accounting for the biological interpretation of the perturbation. To that end, we used GGMs, which were statistical graph models based on partial correlation coefficients. We chose to use a GGM over simple Pearson correlations since correlations were only detected for direct but not indirect dependencies (Krumsiek et al. 2011). Beyond conventional GGM analysis, where one GGM was calculated for the entire data set, we introduced a disease-driven GGM calculation. With this here introduced dGGM approach, we were able to address the question whether a correlation in the GGM was biologically relevant or not. In general, not every identified correlation on the entire dataset was equally relevant to the disease, especially since the majority of the dataset were control measurements. While identifying only those lipids that respond to the biologically relevant perturbations but not to

4.3 Differential Gaussian Graphical Model

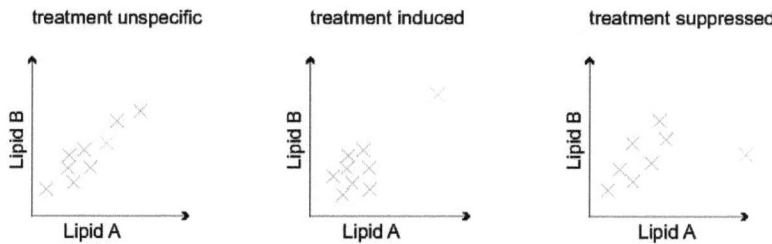

Figure 4.6: Scenarios for Correlations Given a Sample of Interest. For each two components the measurement were plotted per sample. The SOI was marked in orange while the set of CS were marked green. Different scenarios rendered a pairwise correlation unspecific, induced or suppressed by SOI.

control perturbations, we answered the key question: Which lipids or lipid classes were co-affected by the perturbation by wild-type (wt) p53 transfection prior to SN-38 chemotherapy triggering apoptosis of the brain tumor cell lines?

4.3.2 dGGM Design Principle

For the presented dataset, basically one sample out of eight was the only sample effecting the U87 phenotype (Table 4.1). For a given correlation, three fundamental cases were differentiated. Imagine plotting the MS intensity measurements of two variables/lipids of a significant correlation and color-coding the measurements by "sample of interest" (SOI) and "control samples" (CS). Therein, three cases had to be discriminated (Figure 4.6) as described in the following:

Unspecific Correlation. In a general correlation on the entire dataset, SOI and CS contributed equally to a true correlation. Although the SOI itself contributed to the correlation, the correlation was already equally strong on all CS alone. With respect to the SOI, the correlation of the entire dataset was considered unspecific.

Induced Correlation. The correlation on the entire dataset was majorly induced by the SOI, when e.g. the CS had already a tendency to correlate, but were not truly (significantly) correlated. Without the SOI in the dataset, the components were not correlated. With respect to the SOI, the correlation was considered to be induced by the SOI.

Suppressed Correlation. On the entire dataset no true correlation existed for the two components. Closer inspection showed that CS was truly correlated, but lost correlation when calculated together with the SOI. Thus, the correlation gained significance when the SOI was removed from the dataset. With respect to the SOI, the correlation was considered suppressed by the SOI.

4.3.3 dGGM Algorithm

To identify those partial correlations of lipids only resulting from the biologically relevant perturbation and not from side effects of one perturbation, we implemented the following concept of disease-specificity. For simplicity, we name the biologically relevant perturbation "disease" in contrast to the "controls" in the following, although this combination of perturbation is the one inhibiting tumor cell growth. Likewise, the diseased or disease-specific sample was the SOI and the set of all CS were the disease-unspecific controls.

Let S be the set of n samples composed of control and one disease sample $S = (s_1, \ldots, s_n) = (s_D, s_{C_1}, \ldots, s_{C_{n-1}}) = (s_D, s_{C.})$ with the disease sample s_D and the union of all control samples $s_{C.}$. Imagine $\zeta^*(S)$ to be a significant correlation on the entire dataset S. The correlation may then be a result of a perfect correlation of controls not substantially affected by the disease samples or be a result where primarily the disease samples induced a correlation on the entire dataset (controls alone were not correlated). In other words:

4.3 Differential Gaussian Graphical Model

if a correlation has no specific relevance to the disease, we would still detect a correlation when using a truncated dataset with solely control samples.

Those correlations, which were mainly a result of strong CS correlation, were considered "false positive" (FP) with respect to true disease relevance. In order to gather all truly disease-specific correlation, we also had to account for the reverse case, equivalently the "false negatives" (FN) with respect to . If a correlation existed on the control samples s_C, but was suppressed on the entire dataset S, the disease samples do not follow the correlation of the controls, wherein the correlation was again relevant with respect to the disease. This reverse case corresponds to the concept of suppressed variables, which denoted a variable to be a suppressor when suppressing the correlation between some other variable to the remaining variables (Abhimanyu and David 2008, Velicer 1978).

All disease-relevant partial correlations were assessed in an approach inspired by jackknife resampling (Miller 1974). Accordingly, $n + 1$ GGMs were calculated by leaving out one sample from the dataset ($Z^*_{S\setminus s_i}$) during each iteration, resulting in a set of partial correlation coefficients for each lipid pair (l_i, l_j) of $\{\zeta^*(S), \zeta^*(S\setminus s_D), \zeta^*(S\setminus s_{C_1}), \ldots, \zeta^*(S\setminus s_{C_{n-1}})\}$ for all existing significant partial correlations. Figure 4.7 illustrates the approach to build a differential GGM by evaluating the set of leave-one-out GGMs with respect to the criterion of disease-specificity. A pseudo-code formalized the differential GGM approach (Algorithm 4.1).

In detail, we extracted those interactions IA_{ij} of (l_i, l_j) which fulfilled the criterion to be disease-relevant by comparing all GGMs with respect to the disease sample s_D as

$$\text{IA}_{ij} = \begin{aligned}&[\neg \exists \zeta^*(S\setminus s_D) \land \forall_{s_i \in \{S, S\setminus s_{C_.}\}} \exists \zeta^*(s_i)] \\ &\lor [\exists \zeta^*(S\setminus s_D) \land \forall_{s_i \in \{S, S\setminus s_{C_.}\}} \neg \exists \zeta^*(s_i)].\end{aligned}$$

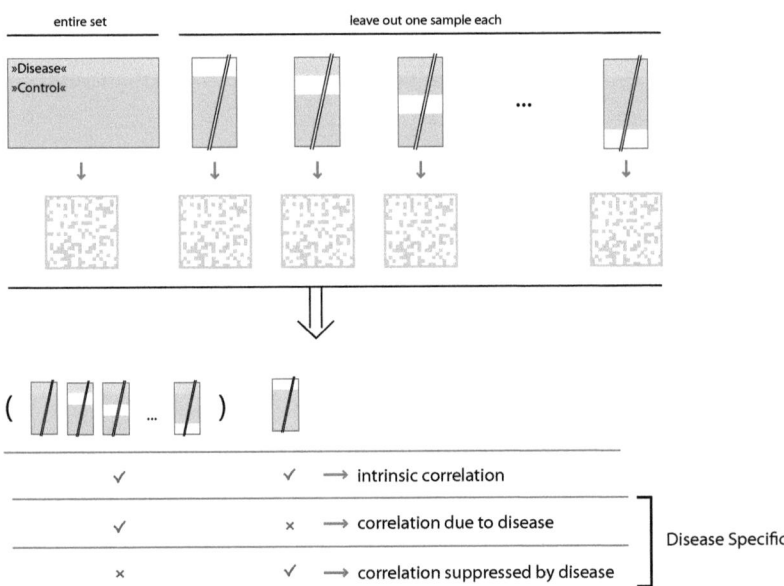

Figure 4.7: dGGM Approach by Jackknife Resampling. To investigate whether a significant partial correlation was specific for the disease sample, partial correlations were calculated for the entire dataset as well as for datasets where each one sample was left out. Unless a correlation is significant in all GGMs, it was considered disease-specific.

4.3 Differential Gaussian Graphical Model

Algorithm 4.1 dGGM

ggm := empty set of GGMs
ggm(0) = result of GGM with S
for i = 1:n **do**
   ggm(i) = result of GGM with S\ Si
end for

dGGM = empty set of differential GGM edges
for all possible edges : e=(l_i,l_j) **do**
   if e fulfills IA_{ij} w.r.t. ggm **then**
     dGGM ∪= e between nodes l_i and l_j
   end if
end for

return dGGM

In other words, we considered an edge disease-specific if it fulfills either one of two criteria: (1) The edge was not significant in the GGM of $S \backslash s_D$, the dataset S without the disease sample s_D, while it was significant in the GGM constructed from the entire dataset S as well as in all GGMs of $S \backslash s_C$ where each one control sample was left out for the calculation. (2) The reverse case holded if the edge was significant on the dataset without the disease sample $(S \backslash s_D)$ – equivalent to a correlation of CS – while the edge was not significant if the disease sample was present in the dataset (that were the datasets of S and any $S \backslash s_C$). As a result, we obtained one differential GGM of only direct lipid-lipid correlations resulting from the combination of wt p53 transfection prior to SN-38 chemotherapy for the Glioblastoma *lipidome*.

4.3.4 dGGM of the Glioblastoma Lipidome

We generated the dGGM for the Glioblastoma *lipidome* according to our jackknife-inspired approach. The FDR cutoff for each calculated GGM value was set to $q = 0.01$. The resulting Gliobastoma-relevant dGGM identified 34 lipid-lipid interactions of 45 lipids from the *lipidome* which were significantly correlated upon p53 gene therapy prior to SN-38 chemotherapy (Figure 4.8).

Since we obtained correlations across all six lipid species, our results were more comprehensive than the results of previous analyses (Görke et al. 2010, He et al. 2010) where lipid species were always handled separately. Compared to conventional GGM applications (c.f. Figure 4.5, analysis of just the entire dataset), we were able to break down each significant correlation with respect to the contribution of each sample.

Qualitative Interpretation of dGGM

Sulfatides are glycosphingolipids with two variable ceramide tails. Sulfatides are also ligands of other Galectins. Out of five measured sulfatides, three (60%) were differentially correlated. The three C31:1, C34:2 and C34:2+O are all short chain ceramides with increased levels for the p53 plus SN-38 perturbation (He et al. 2010). We assigned the C34:2+O sulfatide a more important role with respect to the disease, as it had a prominent role in the differential GGM with five edges. Note, that we revealed the sulfatide regulation only by inspecting the suppressed correlations, which would have been overlooked by conventional GGM analysis.

Gangliosides are glycosphingolipids where one of the two side chains is fixed to a C18:1 fatty acid. They additionally vary in their number of salic acid residues (mono, di or tri). In general, 17 out of 32 (53%) measured gangliosides were co-regulated in the disease-specific GGM. Of the the major gangliosides found in adult brain (GM3/GD3) (Ando and Yu 1984), only one was measured by MS. Interestingly, the GM3 was found to be overrepresented with 61% in the GGM (8 out of 13 measured). As previously shown to have decreased level for the p53 plus SN-38 perturbation (He et al. 2010), the long chain gangliosides GD1 and GM1b were also found to be

4.3 Differential Gaussian Graphical Model

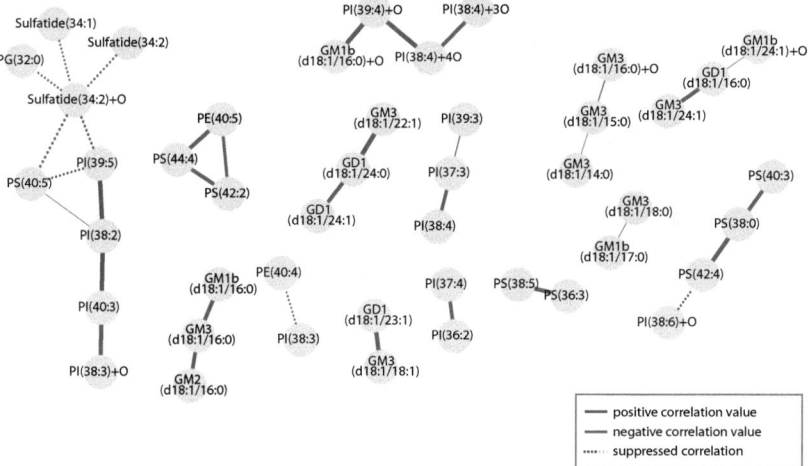

Figure 4.8: Lipids Specifically Correlated. Disease relevant GGM which was associated with the combined perturbation of p53 adenoviral transfection prior to SN-38 chemotherapy in U87 Glioblastoma cell lines. Edges between lipid nodes were drawn if a significant correlation exists. Positive and negative correlations were color-coded in pink and blue, respectively; Suppressed correlations drawn with dotted lines. Edge line widths indicate degree of dependencies (absolute partial correlation value). The numbers C:D indicates the number of carbon atoms (C) and double bonds (D) of the fatty acid side chain(s).

overrepresented in the GGM by 50% (4 of 8) and 66% (4 of 6), respectively. Interestingly, GM1 is a major ligand of Galectin-1.

Besides the two lipid classes which were overrepresented by more than a half of the measured lipids, another interesting lipid class were phosphatidylinositols (PIs). PIs are phospholipids with two esterified fatty acyl residues and inositol as the polar head group. In general, PI are involved in control of cell survival, proliferation and movement. One fourth of the PI were found to be enriched in the GGM (14 of 55). In the original study, the phosphatidylglycerols (PGs) were used as a generic example to show the increased levels of all four phospholipids subclasses (He et al. 2010). Nevertheless, we detected an overrepresentation of PIs. A more detailed biological analysis of the PI may reveal the affected mechanisms.

Disease-relevance of dGGM

To illustrate the advance of a dGGM over a conventional GGM, the fractions of lipid-lipid correlations were classified by disease-specificity with respect to data subset in a confusion matrix. Correlations were classified by being true or false with respect to their disease-specificity while being grouped by occurrence in the correlations in the entire dataset and those being suppressed in the analysis of the entire dataset.

If we examined the *lipidome* solely from the perspective of conventional GGM calculations, we would have obtained 256 significant lipid-lipid correlations (Figure 4.9). With the dGGM approach we found 25 correlations to be disease-relevant with respect to the perturbation of p53 gene therapy prior to SN-38 chemotherapy. In addition, we identified 9 significant lipid-lipid correlations which were suppressed by the disease-relevant sample. Further experimental validation of the dGGM set will be most probably be more successful than choosing lipid correlations from the GGM set.

Surprisingly, less than 10% of all significant interactions of a GGM from the entire dataset were actually disease-specific, or figuratively speaking

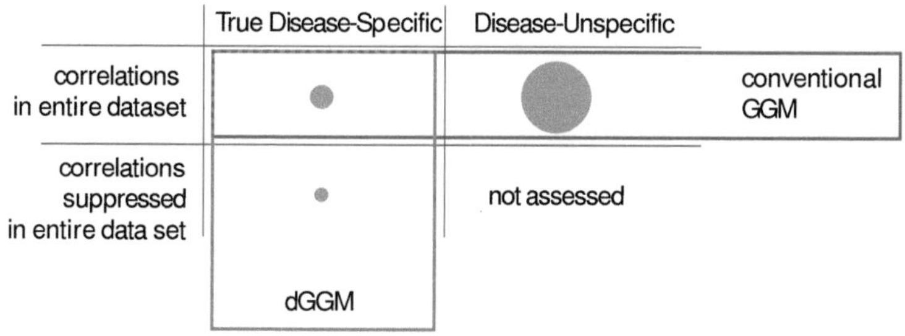

4.3 Differential Gaussian Graphical Model

	True Disease-Specific	Disease-Unspecific	
correlations in entire dataset	●	⬤	conventional GGM
correlations suppressed in entire data set	•	not assessed	
	dGGM		

Figure 4.9: Specific and Unspecific Correlations. Relative number of disease specific (the dGGM) and unspecific lipid-lipid partial correlations. Analysis of the entire dataset was named "conventional" GGM with respect to disease specificity.

"true positive" (TP). Drawing any biological conclusions from correlations on the entire dataset (with ≈ 90 % FP) may therefore be misleading.

Lipid-Lipid Correlation Plots

Closer inspection of actual partial lipid-lipid correlations confirmed prior assumptions on underlying correlation types (c.f. Figure 4.6). The three correlation scenarios of unspecific, induced and suppressed correlation built the dGGM dataset.

Unspecific correlation example was selected from the correlations of the GGM, not present in the dGGM. Intensities of the two gangliosides GM1b C(d18:1/16:0) and GM1b C(d18:1/16:0)+o were significantly correlated (Figure 4.10a). The two measurements of the SOI (highlighted in red) solely strengthened the overall partial correlation while their relevance to the disease was rather low.

The two disease specific correlation types present in the dGGM were induced and suppressed correlations with respect to the SOI. For example, lipids phosphatidylethanolamine (PE) (C40:5) and phosphatidylserine (PS) C(44:4) were uncorrelated on the control samples while the SOI was the

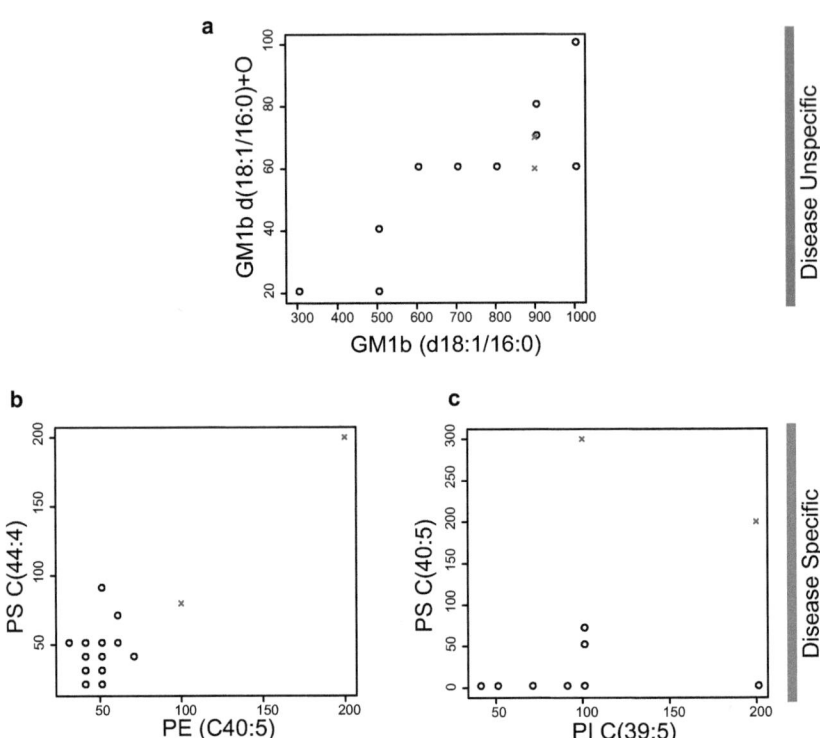

Figure 4.10: Examples of Three Correlation Scenarios for Disease-specific dGGM. a-c. MS/MS measurements of two lipids plotted for each sample. SOI measurements were highlighted with a red cross, control samples with a black circle. **a.** Unspecific correlation for the two lipids were still correlated when SOI was removed for calculations. **b.** Induced correlation for the two lipids where control samples were not correlated but with SOI a correlation was induced. **c.** Suppressed correlation for the two lipids where SOI alone suppressed the correlation of the control samples when analyzing the entire dataset.

4.3 Differential Gaussian Graphical Model

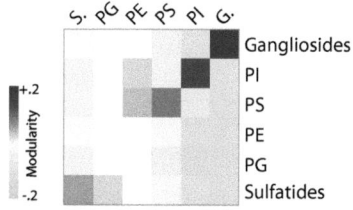

Figure 4.11: Lipids Classes in dGGM. Modularity matrix was calculated by using lipid classes as cluster label for the GGM. Modularity values were color-coded between −0.2 and +0.2 from yellow to blue, respectively. Modularity values close to 1 indicate strong inner-cluster connectivity and little links outside its cluster.

one inducing a significant correlation on the entire dataset (Figure 4.10b). In contrast, lipids PI C(39:5) and PS C(40:5) were correlated on the control samples but not significantly correlated whenever SOI was considered for the calculations (Figure 4.10c).

Lipid Class Modularity of dGGM

Finally, we aimed to analyze the extend to which the lipid classes were interlinked with each other in the disease-specific GGM. We calculated the modularity (here: $m_{ij} = (e_{ij} - a_i^2)$) by considering each lipid class as the node class label (Figure 4.11). We assumed that the lipid classes with little or no links to other classes had a disease-relevant regulation based on their molecular characteristics and were not caused by e.g. fatty acid remodeling. The sulfatides showed the most prominent inner-group linkage, indicating that this class was specifically affected by the p53 plus SN-38 perturbation. The gangliosides and all four phospholipids classes were generally interlinked, indicating that a disease-relevant mechanism was rather linked to common fatty acid side chains than their unique characteristic head groups or affecting the superclass of phospholipids itself.

4.4 Conclusion and Outlook

We have developed a biologically driven technique to analyze high-throughput measurements. The novel method of a dGGM was inspired by the experimental design of the biological study to reveal disease-relevant information. The dGGM was applied to the influence of p53 gene therapy prior to SN-38 chemotherapy on U87 Glioblastoma cell lines. We identified only those lipid correlations which were solely induced by the combined perturbation and not just by a single perturbation. Beyond prior studies of quantification histograms and lipid profiles on single lipid classes, we succeeded in analyzing lipids across their classes for the Glioblastoma *lipidome* which was also easy to comprehend. The disease-specific correlations will advance the understanding of primary brain tumors and their mechanism to immortality.

To advance the molecular understanding of the Glioblastoma phenotype, the dGGM may further be integrated with biological pathway information. For example, edges may be classified by simple combinatoric with respect to the following cases: Was the lipid head group remodeled from one node to another? Was the lipid oxidized? Was there a possible remodeling of attached fatty acids? The question whether a specific enzyme, lipid class or even attached fatty acid were primary targets to maintain immortality remains to be elucidated. The obtained information may then be integrated to current knowledge on lipid metabolism and enzymes catalyzing specific correlations. The dGGM and their biological interpretation will allow to advance the understanding of brain tumorigenesis.

5 Image Pattern Dependencies

A cell's plasma membrane (PM) is a complex mixture of lipids and proteins. The PM is a highly specialized organelle that selectively mediates import and export of a multitude of molecules, while serving as a platform for various signaling complexes. Efficient coordination of these functions may be facilitated by lateral segregation of proteins into distinct domains. Studies on protein and lipid segregation within the plane of the PM is not only experimentally challenging, but also requires careful analysis. To advance the understanding of the PM of living cells beyond synthetic minimal membranes, we systematically studied the lateral distribution of PM proteins in yeast with high resolution fluorescence microscopy. We found that the sole application of standard image analysis techniques was not sufficient to understand the principles of PM protein domain formation as it can be observed in the yeast PM. Thus, we implemented automatic quantification algorithms to assess domain formation and domain co-existence principles. With one-color fluorescence microscopy images, we show that the protein domains formed are more diverse than previously assumed. To quantify the diverse patterns a novel domain distribution coefficient was developed. Domain co-existence has previously been quantified by intensity-based colocalization coefficients of two-color fluorescence images. Interestingly, we found that colocalization depends on the domain pattern formed. Biological interpretation solely of standard analyses would have been misleading.

Our extensive *membrane proteome* analyses with corrections for random expectations enabled us to better understand the mixing behavior of proteins and lipids in the yeast PM.

The part of this chapter on novel findings of the membrane proteome was published with equal contribution of Felix Spira in Spira et al. (2012) and was discussed in more detail in Mueller et al. (2012).

5.1 Biological Question and Data

5.1.1 Membrane Proteome

The "*membrane proteome*" will here be defined as the unification of the proteins associated with the (plasma) membrane, either by integration into the lipid bilayer or by anchorage to lipids. In the PM, proteins and lipids can never be studied without neglecting the effects of the other, since lateral segregation of proteins in the membrane likely depends on their surrounding environment – the lipids – unless actively scaffolded.

5.1.2 Membrane Proteome Analyses Today

In spite of extensive studies, the mechanisms that drive lateral segregation of PM components are still a subject of discussion (Bagatolli et al. 2010, Lingwood et al. 2009). Several competing models explained the emergence of lateral heterogeneities in the distribution of both proteins and lipids in membranes. The lipid-raft theory (Lingwood et al. 2009, Simons and Ikonen 1997) postulated separation of liquid ordered domains enriched in cholesterol and sphingolipids (rafts) from liquid disordered domains mainly containing phospholipids. Rafts were shown to be involved in various processes including intracellular trafficking, signal transduction and cell polarization (Coskun and Simons 2009, Lingwood et al. 2009). Formation of rafts was proposed to depend on inflexible lipids shells surrounding each

5.1 Biological Question and Data

protein (Anderson and Jacobson 2002). Moreover, other scaffold-inducing components were also proposed to influence PM organization, like protein-protein interactions (Charrin et al. 2009, Douglass and Vale 2005), the cortical actin cytoskeleton (Kusumi et al. 1993) and the extracellular matrix (Sackmann et al. 1995). Since the formulation of the fluid mosaic model of membranes (Singer and Nicolson 1972), studies on artificial membranes (minimal synthetic membranes of few lipids and artificial proteins) suggested self-organizing mechanism based on weak interactions between proteins and lipids (Bagatolli et al. 2010, Mouritsen and Bloom 1993). According to these theories on artificial membranes, lateral segregation was considered to be a property of all biological membranes with their inherent diversity of lipids (Ejsing et al. 2009) and proteins.

Protein segregation in the PM of budding yeast *Saccharomyces cerevisiae* was shown to segregate into three non-overlapping domains. First, several amino acid permease (Malínská et al. 2004) were found to cluster with static components called eisosomes in a stable patch-like membrane compartment (membrane compartment marked by Can1/Sur7) (Strádalová et al. 2009, Walther et al. 2006, Young et al. 2002); Second, the major membrane ATPase Pma1 occupied a dense network-like compartment (Malínská et al. 2003); Third, a dynamic patch-like domain was described, which was marked by Tor complex 2 (Berchtold and Walther 2009). Furthermore, several other proteins examined, such as Gap1 and Hxt1, were reported to be homogeneously distributed (Malínská et al. 2003).

5.1.3 The Yeast Plasma Membrane Proteome

Systematic studies of protein localization in biological membranes are currently lacking but will advance the understanding of the mechanisms of lateral segregation. To experimentally uncover the principles underlying PM organization, we have performed a comprehensive characterization of PM protein organization in budding yeast.

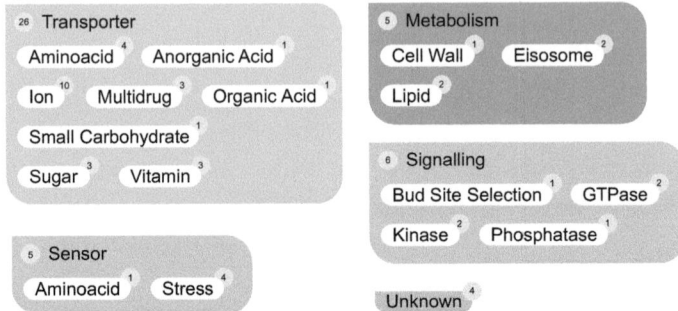

Figure 5.1: PM Protein Classes. The 46 PM proteins chosen for analysis were divided into four subgroups, based on their biological function: transporters, sensors, metabolism and signaling. Four proteins were selected with unknown function. The number of proteins in each group is indicated.

Plasma Membrane Protein Classes

We assembled an exhaustive list of 279 proteins associated with the PM in *S. cerevisiae* from databases and literature. For in depth characterization we selected a set of 46 proteins that included representatives of all major functional categories: transporter, sensor, metabolism and signaling (Figure 5.1).

Imaging of Spatial Patterns

For each representative protein, a strain was generated where the gene of the green fluorescent protein (GFP) was genetically fused to the gene of interest – together encoding a GFP fusion protein. Strains used in our study are the genetic variants of *Saccharomyces cerevisiae*. To study protein localization in the PM of living cell, individual strains (individual GFP fusions) were imaged with Total Internal Reflection Fluorescence (TIRF) microscopy. This technique was optimally suited to studying events at the cell surface, as out-of-focus excitation and photobleaching of fluorophores were minimized (Axelrod et al. 1983) and was applicable to intact plant and yeast cells, although they possess thick cell walls (Sparkes et al. 2011, Uchida et al.

5.1 Biological Question and Data

2011). The yeast PM is flat with only few invaginations at eisosomes (Loibl et al. 2010, Walther et al. 2006) and actin patches (Mulholland et al. 1994). The cell wall also prevents interactions of PM proteins with the overlying coverslip. By combining TIRF microscopy with 2-dimensional (2D) deconvolution techniques (Sund et al. 1999), yeast PM proteins were visualized with high contrast and high temporal resolution.

Deconvolution is an image restoration technique and basically reverts the physical imaging process in which fluorescent objects are characteristically blurred (convolved). In our study, TIRF microscopy images were restored by deconvolution using the classical maximum likelihood estimation algorithm of Huygens Professional 3.4 Software (Scientific Volume Imaging b.v.). Green and red fluorescent latex beads were imaged separately to experimentally determine the point spread function (PSF) for each channel and experimental setting. Roughly 20 beads were averaged to extract the PSFs, which were then used as input for the deconvolution algorithm. With one PSF and one raw microscopy image, the deconvolved image was iteratively restored by minimizing the likelihood that convolution of the deconvolved image (plus a noise function) was identical to the initial raw image, given our measured PSF .

Imaging of Protein Colocalization

An automated data analysis pipeline was established to avoid any unnecessary bias influencing quantification results (Waters 2009). First, cells were automatically detected and extracted from the image data. Since TIRF microscopy visualized only top sections of cells and cell boundaries were not visible, standard cell detection algorithms were inapplicable. For automatic cell detection from our TIRF images, maximum projections of red and green channels were blurred (Gaussian blur) and filtered for noise (median filter) in order to smooth out the spatial patterns to expected cell boundaries. From the preprocessed images, cells were easier to detect by iteratively searching for high intensity peaks in the image before finding the cell boundaries by derivations in x and y directions. Second, the extracted raw images containing just one cell were separately deconvolved in each channel. In addition the beads were also deconvolved. Finally, sub-pixel alignment of deconvolved beads within each image was used to determine the x-y shift of the two filter sets. After shifting the red channel with respect to the beads, each image contained one cell recorded with two independent channels. Each cell in its image was marked with an ellipsoid region of interest (ROI), which was adjusted to the anticipated cell boundaries.

5.2 Quantification of Spatial Patterning

5.2.1 Qualitative Observations

We imaged cells expressing GFP fusions to the representative protein set of the *membrane proteome*. With manual inspection of all cells, we found that all proteins were distributed non-homogeneously. Even proteins previously annotated to cover the entire PM in a homogeneous manner showed network-like patterns. Interestingly, proteins of our *membrane proteome* not only localized in the previously observed distinct patch- or network-like patterns (Berchtold and Walther 2009, Malínská et al. 2003, Young et al. 2002), but also in patterns which appeared to be many intermediate variants (Figure 5.2a). For example, we observed proteins like Bio5 with distinct and equally-distributed patches, Mep2 with mostly patches with few track-like elements or patches in close proximity and Hxt3 with many track-like elements distributed adjacent to patches (Figure 5.2b). Many proteins, such as Hxt3, formed networks that had so far only been reported for Pma1. Notably, lipid-anchored were also not homogeneously distributed but formed equal networks (Gpa1, Ras2 and Psr1).

5.2 Quantification of Spatial Patterning

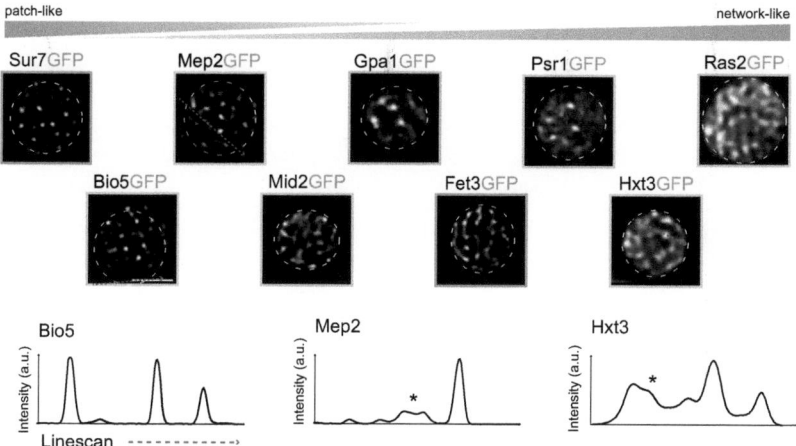

Figure 5.2: Protein Domain Patterns. TIRF microscopy of GFP-labeled PM proteins revealed not only the two basic lateral distribution patterns – patch-like and network-like – but what appeared to be intermediate variations of the two. Representative line scans showed patch- (local maxima) or track-like (marked with asterisks) elements.

5.2.2 Image Quantification by Network Factor

To better assess the pattern diversity, we defined a network-likeness to harbor track-like low intensity elements mostly connected to high-intensity patches in the image and assumed these elements to be generated by proteins below the temporal or spatial resolution.

The existence of fine-granular differences in the domain patterns called for the development of a new algorithm to quantify these images. The quantification was aimed to yield a single numeric factor for each cell's spatial pattern capturing the characteristics. We sought to differentiate between patterns with mostly high-intensity areas (tendency to be patch-like) and patterns with a reasonable fraction of intermediate-intensity areas (tendency to be network-like). The factor ideally should range between cells of "unique patch-like" up to "densely network-like".

Image Pattern Dependencies

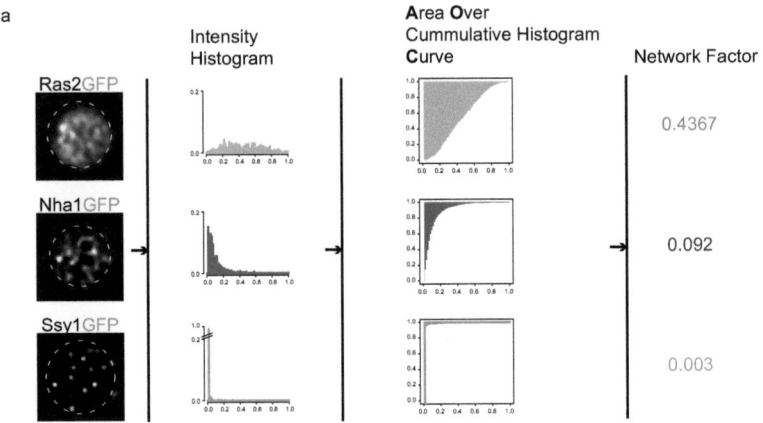

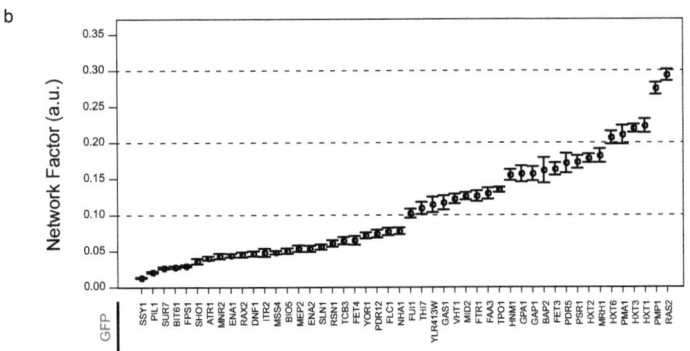

Figure 5.3: Network Factor of Domain Patterns. a. From the image, first, 64-bin intensity histograms were calculated, second, cumulative histograms built and, finally, area over the cumulative histogram curves were sufficient to derive the desired network factor. **b.** Comprehensive protein set was quantified with method from (a.) with $n \leq 10$

5.2 Quantification of Spatial Patterning

To develop the "network factor" quantifying lateral protein domain patterns, we first generated intensity histograms. Histograms were in principle able to capture the desired characteristic: whenever cells had just patches or more and more intermediate intensity values histograms had distinguishable patterns. The number of bins was fixed to 64 while minimal and maximal intensity value were used as lower and upper intensity boundaries, respectively. Thus, intensities $I = (i_{ij})$ of the ROI of a cell in x and y were used to generate the 64 bin counts for the histogram $H = (h_i)$ with $1 \leq i \leq 64$ and h_i the number of pixels in I of respective intensity value falling in the range of h_i. Three sample proteins were selected to visualize the differences in their histograms for a patch-, an intermediate and a network-like pattern (Figure 5.3a).

The idea to yield one factor for one entire histogram for one cell was to first generate a cumulative histogram $C = (c_i)$ with $c_i = \sum_{j=1}^{i} h_j$. Already conceivable from the cumulative histograms in Figure 5.3a, a single network factor may be calculated from C by e.g. the area over the curve. The new network factor nf was subsequently defined as

$$\text{nf}(I) = \sum_{i=1}^{64} c_i$$

When calculating the network factor for each cell for each labeled protein (45 proteins with $n \geq 10$) the domain patterns visible from the initial manual qualitative study were nicely preserved with the network factor (Figure 5.3b). The protein Sur7 and Pma1 – described to form a patch- and network-like pattern respectively – were ranging in the outer spectrum of the nf values. Interestingly, proteins, like Pmp1 (the regulatory peptide of Pma1) and Ras2 (lipid anchored Rho-GTPase) form even stronger networks than Pma1 itself. The protein Ssy1 (amino acid sensor) showed an even more distinct patch-like pattern. Note, that the factor was named network factor while network-like values of nf → 0 indicated a patch-like pattern, thus, without track-like (intermediate intensity values) elements in the image.

5.3 Sole Pairwise Dependence

We next aimed to elucidate domain compositions. We defined a domain as the total membrane area occupied by a particular protein. To this end, we performed colocalization experiments with pairs of GFP and red fluorescent protein (RFP) fusions using two-color TIRF microscopy and (red and green) channel-specific 2D deconvolution. To reliably quantify colocalization we adjusted incidence angles separately for each channel and automated cell detection and image alignment. ROIs were selected for both red and green channels resulting in $R = (r_{ij})$ and $G = (g_{ij})$ intensity values according to I of one-color images.

5.3.1 Quantification Coefficients

To measure the dependence between the red and green protein domains with respect to their spatial constrains, two coefficients were available.

Pearson Correlation Coefficients measures the dependence of both channels by favoring intensity value with little absolute variation as

$$r_{pearson}(R, G) = \frac{\sum (R_i - R_{avg})(G_i - G_{avg})}{\sqrt{\sum (R_i - R_{avg})^2 \sum (G_i - G_{avg})^2}}.$$

The disadvantage of the Pearson correlation was the inability to differentiate absolute intensity values. In other words, the Pearson correlation treats intensity variations around the background signal the same as in high intensity areas.

5.3 Sole Pairwise Dependence

In our experimental setup, however, we expect high spatial colocalization of proteins to be large when high-intensity areas overlap. To account for the actual intensity value and inducing higher colocalization values for overlap of high-intensity areas the Manders overlap coefficient was chosen to quantify domain dependencies (Manders et al. 1993).

Manders Overlaps measures the ratio of intersecting to total object volume as

$$r_{overlap}(R, G) = \frac{\sum R_i G_i}{\sqrt{\sum R_i^2 \sum G_i^2}}.$$

The Manders overlap was sensitive to background signals and unequal intensities in the two channels. Both of these issues were addressed as follows. To account only for colocalization of cell signals but not background, the ROI was manually adjusted for each cell always excluding any background signal. The intensity values inside each ROI per channel was scaled to the entire 8-bit range for equal weighting of both channels (identical intensity range).

In summary, the Manders overlap measured statistical dependency of the intensities originating from two channels and was thus more suitable for quantifying correlations between spatial patterns than the Pearson correlation, which accounted only for intensity variations between channels. We, thus, implemented a colocalization coefficient based on the Manders overlap (Manders et al. 1993, Zinchuk and Grossenbacher-Zinchuk 2009).

5.3.2 Linearization of Manders Coefficient

We systematically evaluated the Manders overlap by generating images mimicking domain patterns (Figure 5.4a) to understand the behavior and scaling of the coefficient. The calculated Manders overlap was plotted against our expected colocalization value and was found to scale with the square root of our expected value (Figure 5.4b). We therefore defined a linear colocaliza-

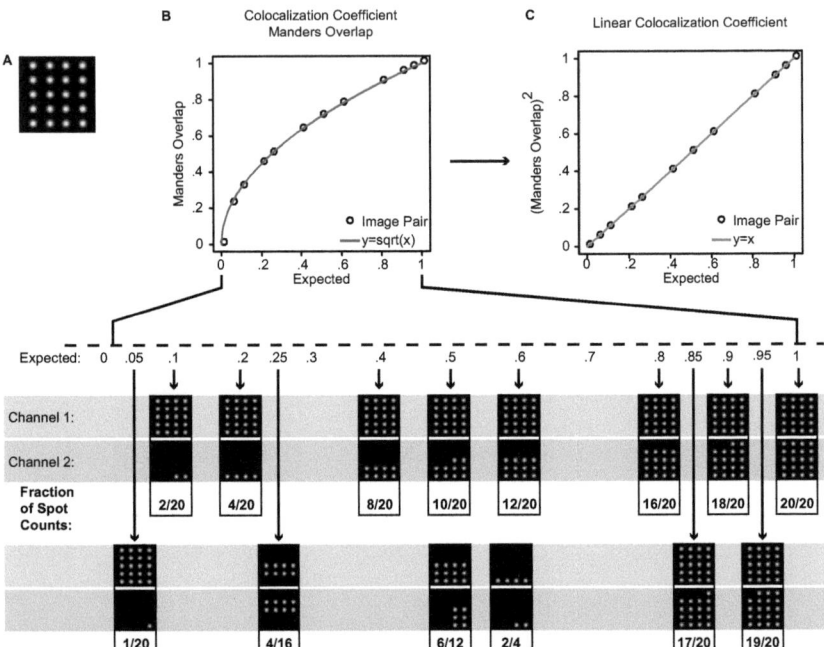

Figure 5.4: Linear colocalization coefficient. a. Synthetic images were generated to mimic patch-like patterns as visualized with false colors. Individual dots were generated with a Gaussian blur. **b.** To evaluate the behavior of the colocalization overlap (according to Manders), several domain overlaps were benchmarked. We defined our expected colocalization value as the fraction of patches common to both channels. For all image pairs the Manders overlap was calculated. We found that the Manders overlap scaled as the square root of our expected colocalization value (red fitted curve). **c.** A linearly scaling colocalization coefficient was then calculated by squaring the Manders overlap (green fitted curve). This squared colocalization coefficient was used throughout our study.

5.3 Sole Pairwise Dependence

tion coefficient (value between 0 and 1) by simply squaring of the Manders overlap (Figure 5.4c):

$$c(R, G) = r_{overlap}(R, G)^2$$

This colocalization coefficient c was used throughout the study and is in the remainder referred to as the colocalization coefficient.

5.3.3 Numerous PM Protein Domains

We first compared the representative *membrane proteome* (fused to GFP) to Sur7 and Pma1 as markers (fused to RFP) for the two previously identified non-overlapping domains (Malínská et al. 2003, Young et al. 2002). The entire *membrane proteome* appeared to be excluded from eisosomes marked by Sur7 (Figure 5.5, dark blue values), except for the known eisosomal component Pil1, based on the overal low colocalization coefficients. The plasma membrane ATPase Pma1 colocalized to various degrees with the representative *membrane proteome* (Figure 5.5, light blue values). The highest colocalization coefficients were observed for functionally related proteins such as Pmp1 (regulator of Pma1), Pdr5 (another ATPase) or Mrh1 (unknown function, but may participate in the Pma1 regulation (Wu et al. 2000)) and lipid anchored proteins Ras2 and Gpa1. Notably, we also found proteins forming stark networks (large network factor), such as Fet3, excluded from the Pma1 domain. These finding already argue against the current yeast PM picture of only two mutually exclusive and stable domains. The only described network-like domain of Pma1 does not comprise all our observed patch- and network-like proteins.

Since most of the examined proteins colocalized only little with the two yeast domain markers, we expanded our domain overlap comparisons. We chose four proteins with low colocalization values with Pma1 or Sur7 and tested them against a smaller subset of the *membrane proteome* (Figure 5.5,

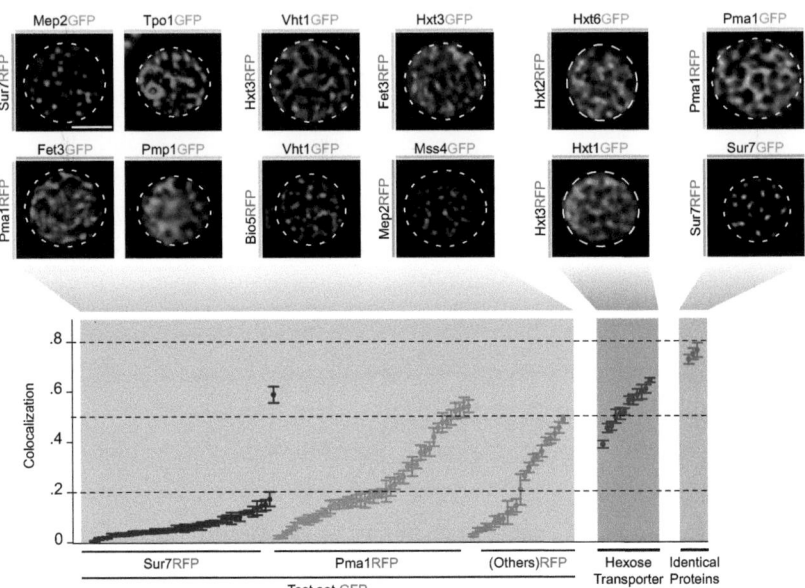

Figure 5.5: Co-existence of Numerous Domains. Two-color TIRF microscopy images of PM proteins (as GFP and RFP fusions). Individual examples of pairwise colocalization were shown in TIRF images. Colocalization coefficients for all proteins examined in this survey (mean ± standard error) were grouped and sorted with respect to the RFP protein labeled. Scale bar 2 μm.

gray values). Again, the measured pairwise domain overlaps ranked with low colocalization coefficients. One reason for the overall low colocalization values may lie in the functional diversity of our selected representative membrane proteome. To further test, whether functional similarity facilitates colocalization, we chose two high- (Hxt2, Hxt6) and two low-affinity (Hxt1, Hxt3) representatives from among the 20 hexose transporters known in budding yeast for pairwise colocalization experiments (Figure 5.5, purple values). All four had also large network factors. We observed higher degrees of colocalization for the hexose transporters than for functionally unrelated protein tested so far – however still lower than for identical proteins (Figure 5.5, red values).

Our extensive colocalization screen revealed that a large number of co-existing domains exists in the yeast PM with every possible overlap degree. These results clearly argue against the currently accepted view of the yeast PM that all integral PM proteins localize to two stable and mutually exclusive domains.

5.4 Non-Random Dependence Measure

We found that all proteins formed co-existing domains with any possible overlap degrees. The biological explanations behind this result, however, remains to be elucidated. To address what rules administer protein segregation into these numerous co-existing domains we compared the colocalization values to random expectations.

5.4.1 Minor Dependence on Intensities

We first evaluated whether the colocalization values were solely a function of the pixel intensity values and independent of the pattern formed. To this end, for each cell analyzed a scrambled cell was generated. Within the ROI

a

b

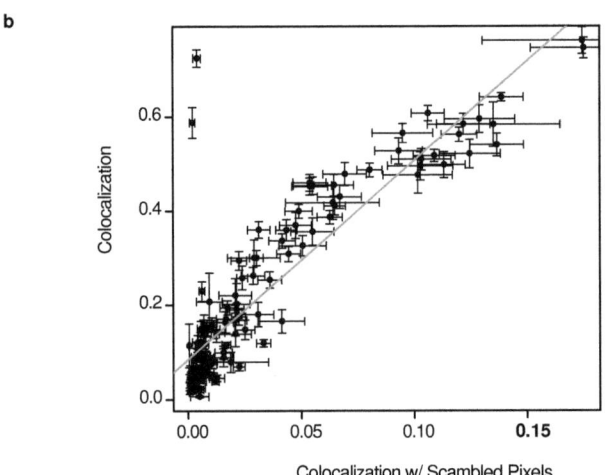

Figure 5.6: Colocalization Versus Scrambled Intensity Values. a. The intensity values from a cell ROI were randomly shuffled independently for each channel resulting in scrambled cells. **b.** Colocalization values were correlated to their random value with a correlation coefficient of 0.87 (p-value 0.0). Deviation were standard errors for each strain. Gray line is the linear regression.

5.4 Non-Random Dependence Measure

used for colocalization analysis, the intensity values were gathered, uniformly shuffled and placed back into the image (Figure 5.6a)

For the each colocalization value one corresponding scrambled colocalization value was calculated. The values were correlated for each strain. The colocalization value was found to be correlated with the one obtained by scrambling the pixel values per channel (Figure 5.6b). Although the pairwise domain overlap significantly depended on the pixels intensities in each channel, the colocalization was no solely explained with the raw values. More specifically, the scrambled colocalization had overlap values of at most 0.2 while the real domain overlap reached average values up to 0.8. The linear model of $c(R, G)$ explained by $c_{scrambled}(R, G)$ is

$$c(R, G) = 0.09 + 4.22 \; c_{scrambled}(R, G)$$

To conclude, the observed colocalization coefficients depended roughly to 23.70 % on the intensity distribution itself but did not allow to fully explain domain overlaps.

5.4.2 Major Dependence on Domain Pattern

Principle of Channel Decoy

To further investigate the hint at a random nature of protein colocalization we chose to generate cells with decoy channels instead of decoy pixels. To that end cells from each strain were gathered (Figure 5.7a) and their red and green channels were shuffled in such a way that decoy-channel cells (cells with non-matching R-G channels) were generated (Figure 5.7b). More specifically, while keeping one channel of one cell fixed, iteratively red channels of all other cells were used to always generate a new decoy cells. The decoy cell's ROI was adjusted to enclose the spatial pattern of both channels by centering and aligning the ROIs of both channels: The centers of both

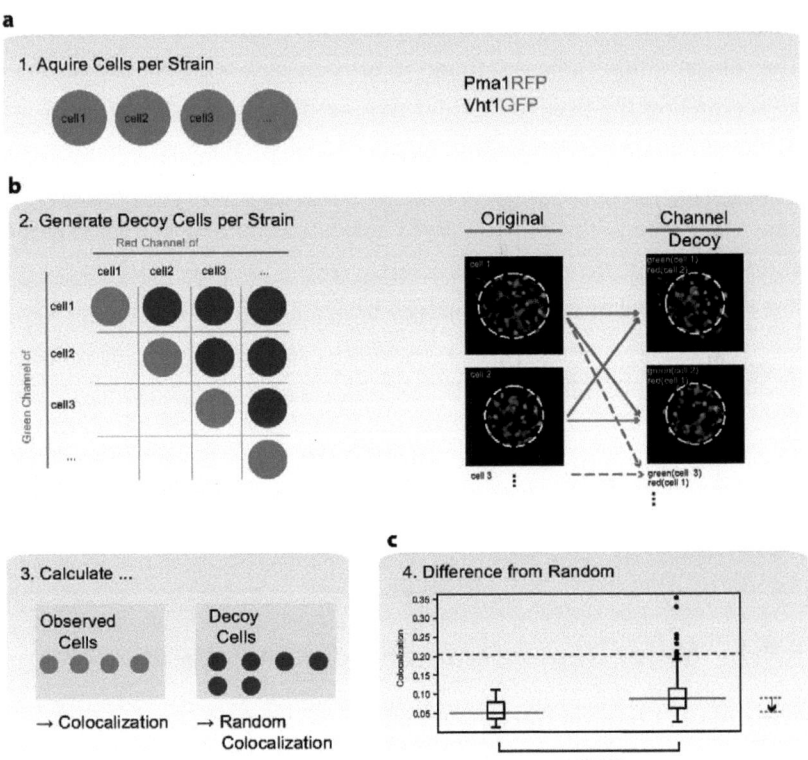

Figure 5.7: Decoy Channels. a. Strains were imaged and cells with red and green channel were prepared for analysis. **b.** Red and green channels of all cells were split and iteratively merged again to mimic random cells. By principle, the originally observed cells were maintained by merging channels of the same cell. **c.** A two-sided t-test can determine whether the set of observed cells differed significantly from the decoy cells. Mean values of both set determine if non-random colocalization is better or worse than random.

5.4 Non-Random Dependence Measure

Table 5.1: Proteins with Non-random Colocalization. Protein with red (RFP) and green (GFP) fluorescent tag. Their colocalization coefficient was $c(R,G)$ with its absolute difference to the channel decoy colocalization value of the strain. Sign of difference indicates if colocalization was better or worse than random. P-value evaluated statistical strength of the colocalization difference.

Direction	*RFP	–	*GFP	$c(R,G)$	$\Delta c(R,G)$	p-value
better	Fet3	–	Fet3	0.7613	0.2080	0.000046
better	Hxt1	–	Hxt3	0.5654	0.1227	0.000046
better	Hxt2	–	Hxt1	0.4598	0.0604	0.002842
better	Hxt2	–	Hxt6	0.5845	0.0763	0.003003
better	Hxt3	–	Fet3	0.4548	0.0626	0.012419
better	Hxt3	–	Hnm1	0.4867	0.0434	0.006596
better	Hxt3	–	Hxt1	0.6417	0.0410	0.000221
better	Hxt3	–	Hxt2	0.4519	0.0539	0.008063
better	Hxt6	–	Hxt1	0.5625	0.0503	0.003637
better	Hxt6	–	Hxt2	0.6076	0.0846	0.000014
better	Pma1	–	Mrh1	0.4780	0.1068	0.000193
better	Pma1	–	Nha1	0.1948	0.0324	0.043281
better	Pma1	–	Pma1	0.7458	0.1912	0.000003
better	Pma1	–	Yor1	0.1903	0.0358	0.021657
better	Sur7	–	Bio5	0.0606	0.0270	0.021729
better	Sur7	–	Fui1	0.1219	0.0510	0.045337
better	Sur7	–	Pil1	0.5879	0.5809	0.000000
better	Sur7	–	Sur7	0.7241	0.7050	0.000000
worse	Pma1	–	Fet3	0.1657	−0.1048	0.001870
worse	Pma1	–	Pil1	0.0214	−0.0251	0.001137
worse	Pma1	–	Sur7	0.0203	−0.0131	0.049219
worse	Pma1	–	Vht1	0.0544	−0.0405	0.000073
worse	Sur7	–	Dnf1	0.0800	−0.0342	0.031586
worse	Sur7	–	Fet3	0.0331	−0.0250	0.000719
worse	Sur7	–	Fps1	0.0154	−0.0110	0.029956
worse	Sur7	–	Mid2	0.0394	−0.0173	0.001747
worse	Sur7	–	Mrh1	0.0492	−0.0436	0.000044
worse	Sur7	–	Nha1	0.0489	−0.0181	0.016688
worse	Sur7	–	Pdr5	0.0594	−0.0366	0.031031
worse	Sur7	–	Pma1	0.0392	−0.0434	0.000002
worse	Sur7	–	Pmp1	0.0694	−0.0609	0.000000
worse	Sur7	–	Ras2	0.1194	−0.0546	0.000001
worse	Sur7	–	Rsn1	0.0411	−0.0175	0.018807
worse	Sur7	–	Sho1	0.0182	−0.0103	0.015931
worse	Sur7	–	Ssy1	0.0064	−0.0062	0.013642
worse	Sur7	–	Tcb3	0.0191	−0.0176	0.000331
worse	Sur7	–	Tpo1	0.0455	−0.0374	0.000015

ROIs were used to determine the shift between images and the corresponding decoy ROI was automatically selected where ROIs of both original cells overlapped.

With the actual observed cells and the respective decoy cells at hand for each strain, we assessed whether the colocalization coefficient occurred by chance or not. If the colocalization was purely random, any channel recombination also may generate the observed colocalization coefficient.

Little Non-Random Colocalization

With the populations of observed and decoy cells, statistical testing allowed to determine whether the observed colocalization value was different from random (Figure 5.7d).

Out of 125 strains, 37 were significantly different from their random value (Table 5.1). All strains, where one protein population was simultaneously tagged with GFP and RFP (one endogenous, one plasmid expression), had all colocalization values better than random. Similarly, seven of the twelve colocalization values of the hexose transporters were significantly better than random. Both low and high affinity transporter (Hxt1-Hxt3 as well as Hxt2-Hxt6, respectively) were significantly independent of their fluorophore tagging. Moreover, the protein Bio5 (uptake of biotin precursor) and Fui1 (uridine permease) not so far associated with eisosomes showed unexpected (better than random) colocalization. Interestingly, their absolute colocalization value was very low. If only the absolute colocalization values were used to determine the overlap with eisosomes, these protein would have been falsely marked to be excluded from eisosomes. Since specialized eisosomes were spatially static and topologically invaginated membrane structures, as many as 14 proteins were found to be excluded (worse than random) in addition to the mutual exclusive domain of Pma1.

5.4 Non-Random Dependence Measure

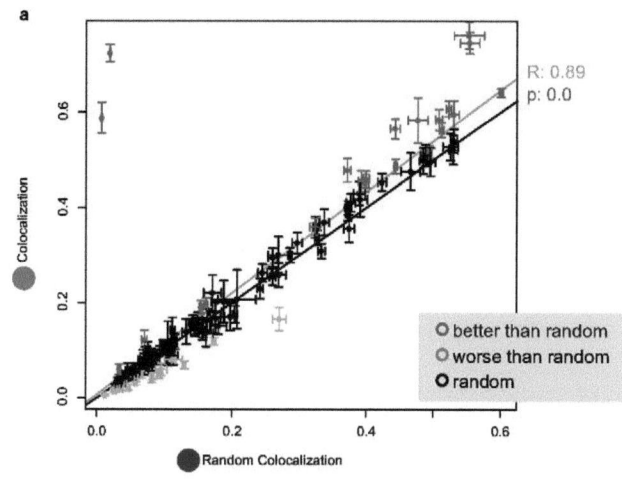
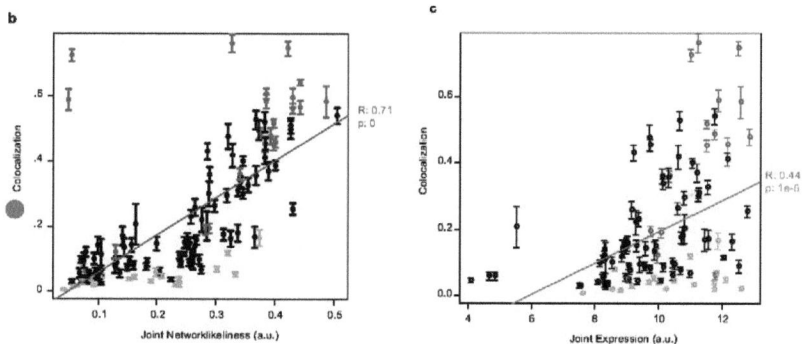

Figure 5.8: Non-Random Colocalization Determined by Network factor. a. Observed and Decoy Colocalization values correlated with a Pearson coefficient of $R = 0.89$ (orange line, p-value=0.0). Black line indicates identity of $c(R_i, G_i) = c_{decoy}(R_{j \neq i}, G_i)$. **b.** Observed colocalization correlated with sum of network factor of (R_i, G_i) (Pearson R=0.71, p-value=0.0, orange line). **c.** Little correlation of colocalization with sum of expression of both (R_i, G_i) (Pearson R=0.44, p-value=$1e-6$, gray line) **a-c.** Protein colocalizations better and worse than randomly expected were colored in magenta and cyan, respectively.

127

Mostly Random Colocalization

Observed and decoy colocalization values were next correlated (Figure 5.8a). Interestingly, the decoy colocalization strongly correlated with the observed colocalization values (correlation coefficient: 0.89, p-value: 0.0). The linear model of the observed colocalization coefficient $c(R_i, G_i)$ and the decoy colocalization $c_{decoy}(R_{j \neq i}, G_i)$ revealed practically a one-to-one effect

$$c(R_i, G_i) = 0.01 + 1.06\, c_{decoy}(R_{j \neq i}, G_i)$$

per strain (R-G protein combination).

To further investigate whether the colocalization was directly dependent on either the abundance or spatial pattern of both protein, colocalization values were also correlated with either values. Abundance and network factor of the proteins were available for only one protein, while colocalization was a coefficient for always two proteins. For calculating joint abundance or network factor of two proteins together, individual values of both proteins were simply summed up before correlated with the observed colocalization values (Figure 5.8b and c, respectively). Note, multiplication of both values yielded lower correlation values. The protein expression did not influence colocalization values as severely as the spatial pattern formed (as measured by network factors).

Random Colocalization Driven by Network Factor

Finally, we aimed to manipulate the generation of the channel decoy cells in order to evaluate wether the perfect correlation may be artificially reduced. To that end, respective decoy cells of each strain were not generated by shuffling channels within each strain, but rather direct channel selection by picking a channel with a network factor that was differed from the observed value – given an "error". For sampling the network factor errors Δnf with differences up to 0.2, overall correlations were calculated for observed

5.4 Non-Random Dependence Measure

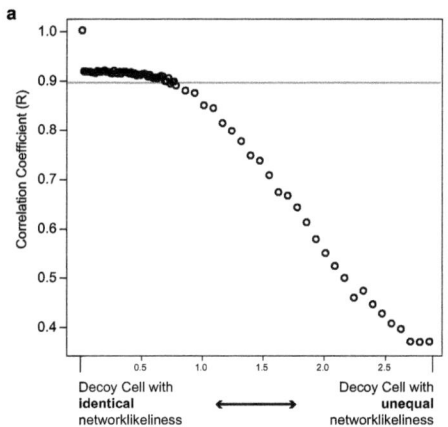

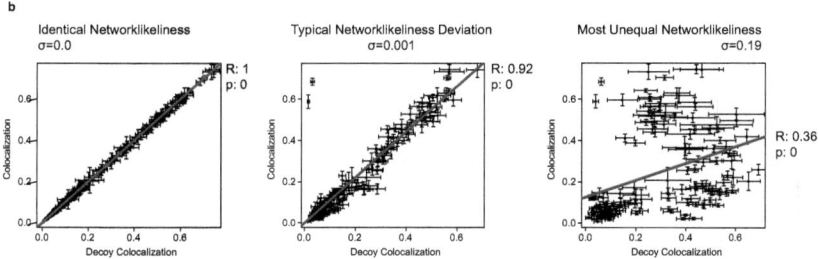

Figure 5.9: Colocalization Driven by Domain Patterns. a. Pearson correlation for varying the error of network factor to the strains characteristic value. Orange line indicated Pearson correlation value for generating decoy cells within one strain. **a.** Exemplary correlations shown for network factors different from the cells value by (σ = 0, 0.001, 0.19).

to respective decoy colocalization (Figure 5.9a). The correlation of observed and decoy cells got indeed constantly lost from identical to most different network factors (Figure 5.9b). This correlation drop demonstrated that the network factor directly affected colocalization values. Thus, random colocalization was a function of its domain pattern and not necessarily the pairwise properties of the protein.

5.5 Conclusion and Outlook

We developed a set of new approaches for fluorescence microscopy analyses. In order to search for underlying principles driving the segregation of the yeast plasma *membrane proteome* we implemented not only an automatic quantification adapting the gradually different spatial patterns but also systematically evaluated protein domain overlaps when compared to artificial random cells. The new approaches revealed that the *membrane proteome* was spatially distributed in numerous co-existing domains, which in turn were mostly subjected to random overlaps induced by their formed spatial patterns.

To further elucidate whether and which factors mechanistically determine random or active domain formation, a variety of experiments and in-depth analyses may be conducted. Domain patterns may be artificially altered by adding drugs or generating gene knockouts altering e.g. lipid composition of the PM. The subsets of random or active pairwise protein segregation may be further evaluated for e.g. sequence similarity, functional relationships or directed scaffolding (e.g. PPI). The presented novel approaches to analyze fluorescent microscopy images will be valuable tools to elucidate the driving mechanism of *membrane proteome*'s mixing behavior.

6 Independent Source Separation

Real datasets were usually solely a record of an observation yielded through experimental means. The actual source processes were, however, not always equal to the observed data, whereas the observations were actually composed of a mixture of various processes without any knowledge on their mixing behaviors. For instance, a protein distribution underlies many individual processes, like modification, binding or translocation, but only the bulk of all protein states was observable within one cell. To reveal their underlying dynamics, proteins were visualized by fluorescence microscopy resulting in multiple *cytome* time series. Typically, protein dynamics were analyzed by fluorescence recovery after photobleaching (FRAP) which basically recorded spatial protein redistributions but mixed with any noise sources. To again de-mix protein behaviors from noise sources after imaging, we chose to use the source separation with Independent Component Analysis (ICA) for the multidimensional images of single FRAP events. The noise-robust ICA-variant FRAP was employed to detect the independent source signals of FRAP datasets. FRAP experiments of the dynamic master regulator of cell polarity Cdc42 were subjected to our ICA analyses. We were able to show that SAM-SOBI was not only generally applicable to FRAP datasets but was also effectively de-mixing FRAP events better than other ICA variants. The ICA variant SAM-SOBI was successfully recovering independent protein processes and noise sources from FRAP data in a noise-robust manner.

Parts of this chapter were published in collaboration with Fabian Theis, who also developed the SAM-SOBI method. Biological experiments used in this chapter were conducted by Tina Freisinger in the lab of Roland Wedlich-Söldner.

6.1 Biological Question and Data

6.1.1 Cytomes

Cytomics aims to understand the collection of all dynamic cellular processes and functions on single cell level (*cytome*) and is usually combined with computational biology (Valet et al. 2004). Fluorescence microscopy *in vivo* allowed to visualize localization of proteins labeled with a fluorescence molecule. For example, proteins may be fused to the green fluorescent protein (GFP) allowing to record the spatial and temporal distribution of the GFP fusion protein, therein the native spatial and temporal organization of the protein of interest. Quantitative measurements of these fluorescent molecules allowed to deepen the understanding of dynamic cellular processes and functions at sub-cellular resolution.

6.1.2 Cytome Source Recovery

Protein localizations were usually recorded by using image snapshots or time-lapse movies (assembly of successive snapshots), but their analyses was limited when underlying dynamic processes, such as protein mobilities, were to be identified. To better understand the general mobility of the spatial and temporal distribution of proteins within single cells, special microscopy techniques like FRAP were used.

6.1 Biological Question and Data

Any protein's dynamics at cellular level was always a mixture of all distribution of protein states at the cellular space in time. To a given time-point a snapshot allowed to determine the spatial distribution of a protein, while only successive snapshots induced the temporal dimension. FRAP is a technique to extract protein mobility information from how fluorescence recovered after irreversible photobleaching (Waters 2009): An intense and focused illumination of a region of interest (ROI) irreversibly photo-bleaches fluorophores in the ROI to a black stage. The protein (im)mobility was then measured by how much intensity recovered within the ROI. More specifically, mobile proteins were locally exchanged in such a way that unbleached molecules entered the ROI while the irreversibly bleached molecules left and subsequently recovering the fluorescence – whereas immobile proteins never left the ROI and no exchange with the unbleached molecules took place, thus, the ROI remained without fluorescence.

Quantification of microscopy images faced several technical challenges (Waters 2009): Measured fluorescence intensities resulted not only from the exited fluorophores but also added up with background signals and intensities from single fluorophores or autofluorescence of e.g. cell cytosol or growth medium. This noise caused intensity fluctuations in addition to successive photo-bleaching of exited fluorophores. For further analyses, these factors must be subtracted from the measured intensities.

6.1.3 Yeast Cdc42 Cytome Establishing Polarization

Cdc42 is a highly conserved master regulator and key mediator of cell polarization and has up to 80% sequence similarity to higher Eukaryotes. In the budding yeast, Cdc42 localizes at the site of polarized growth and is dynamically maintained by various processes. As a plasma membrane-associated small GTPase, Cdc42 cycles between an active and an inactive state. Its active state is bound to a variety of effector proteins to regulate cellular responses, such as cell proliferation, cell cycle progression and rearrangement

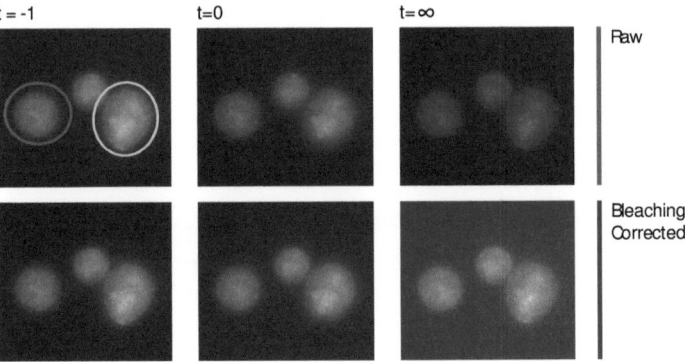

Figure 6.1: Cdc42 FRAP Experiments. Time-lapse movies of Cdc42 fused to GFP were obtained for single FRAP experiments. Three time-points at FRAP-relative time-points (t) before (-1), at (0) and convergence (∞). Since fluorescence was successively lost due to photo-bleaching in the raw movie (**a**), bleaching effects were corrected bases on a reference cell (circled in blue) resulting in bleaching corrected movie (**b**). The cells forming a polarization cap were objected to irreversible photo-bleaching (circled in yellow).

of the actin cytoskeleton. Furthermore, Cdc42 rapidly exchanges between cap and cytosol in a dynamic manner (Wedlich-Soldner et al. 2004).

At the G1/S transition of the cell cycle, Cells start to polarize and initiate bud formation with a cap on the site of polarized growth, eventually growing a bud and subsequently giving birth to a daughter cell. As a master regulator of bud formation, Cdc42 accumulates in a cap on the plasma membrane. The Cdc42 dynamics were studied in the polarization cap by FRAP experiments.

GFP-Cdc42 fusion protein was endogenously expressed in *Saccharomyces cerevisiae* yeast cells and imaged with standard light microscopy. The Cdc42 protein population was visualized in cell cross-sections. Time-lapse movies were each assembled from over 100 snapshots of an individual yeast cell (Figure 6.1a). Intensities of the "FRAP cell" (the cell objected to a FRAP event) were corrected with the intensity decay of a control cell (Figure 6.1b) and further subtracted by the image's background intensity. These corrections were performed prior to data analysis.

FRAP datasets were generated by measuring the Cdc42 fluorescence in the polarized cap, whereby the cap itself was irreversibly bleached at timepoint $t = 0$ (subject of FRAP event). After 25 seconds the fluorescence of the cap almost fully recovered.

6.2 Manual FRAP Curve Fitting

To quantify protein recovery from FRAP experiments, automatic routines were implemented according to Snapp et al. (2003), Sprague and McNally (2005). Three polygon ROIs had to be manually assigned for each FRAP experiment: 1. Reference cell ROI_{ref} to correct for fluorescence bleaching over time. 2. Background ROI_{bg}. 3. Area of bleaching event ROI_{frap}. The ROI_{frap} contained the information used to infer protein dynamics (Figure 6.2a).

Intensity values of each ROI were averaged in each time frame. Background intensities were subtracted from both ROI_{ref} and ROI_{frap}. Fluorescence bleaching $I_{loss}(t)$ over time t was approximated with the ROI_{ref} (divided by their pre-FRAP average intensity). Thus, the FRAP-curve $y_{frap}(t)$ was calculated from ROI_{frap}/I_{loss} and normalized to a range $(0, 1)$ with 0 being the intensity value at the FRAP event and 1 being the average value of $t < 0$ (Figure 6.2b). The y_{frap} curve was then fitted with an exponential distribution function as

$$y_{fit}(t) = a(1 - b(e^{-tc})).$$

From the fit $y_{fit}(t)$, halftimes $t_{1/2}$ can be calculated with $t_{1/2} = -\log 0.5/c$. Mobile fractions were derived from $Mf = a$. Time information was automatically extracted from timestamps saved to the image meta data provided by the acquisition software. Results were only considered for analysis, if the recovery curve yielded a stable plateau within the time of analysis, the fit reliably approximated the raw data (residual sum of squares > 0.95) and the residuals were randomly distributed below and above the curve.

6.2.1 Source Recovery of FRAP with SAM-SOBI

To replace the evaluation-intensive and careful manual FRAP analysis pipeline, we instead employed a robust implementation of the ICA. ICA aimed to reveal underlying source signals of complex processes, such as complex recycling process of Cdc42 in the cap during polarity establishment. We applied the noise-robust ICA variant SAM-SOBI (Theis et al. 2010) and evaluated whether ICA was applicable for evaluating protein mobilities of *cytome* studies.

Multidimensional biomedical imaging required robust statistical analyses. Corresponding experiments, such as FRAP, resulted in multiple time series for each position in the cell. These data were classically characterized by recording response patterns to any kind of stimulation mixed with any degree of noise levels. The temporal auto-decorrelation of SAM-SOBI was aimed to generally detect the underlying signal sources, such as these experimental responses in an unbiased fashion.

SAM-SOBI (Theis et al. 2010) used scatter matrices to estimate the co-variance matrix assuming multivariate normal distributions. For robust data centering a spatial median was applied instead of using a marginal median on each dimension. After centering, a spatial sign auto-covariance matrix (SAM) was used as a robust estimation of the auto-covariances.

6.2.2 Benchmarking FRAP Analyses With SAM-SOBI

SAM-SOBI was applied to the microscopy dataset of Cdc42 FRAP experiments. To benchmark SAM-SOBI performance especially for recovery of

6.2 Manual FRAP Curve Fitting

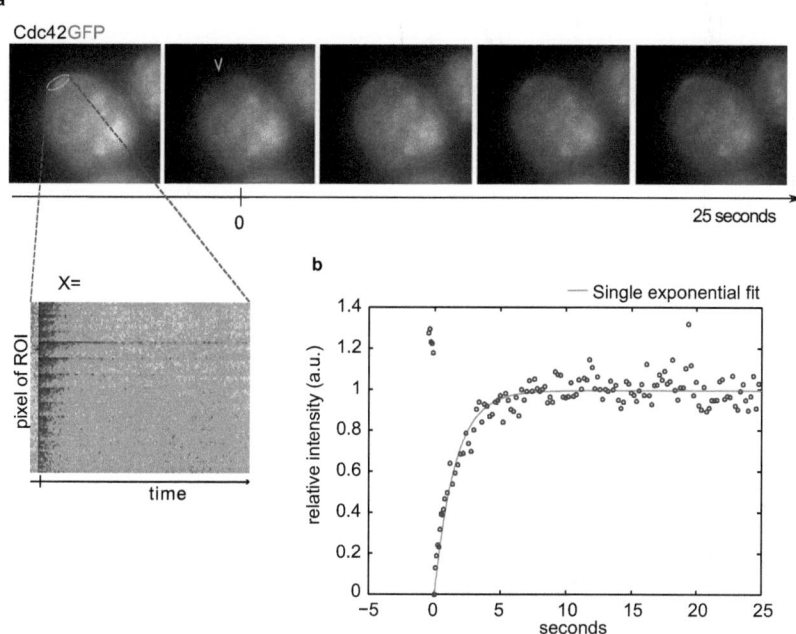

Figure 6.2: FRAP Analysis of Cdc42 Enriched in Caps During Yeast Cell Cycle. The protein Cdc42 fused to GFP was irreversibly photo-bleached during polarization cap formation. **a.** Fluorescence recovery was recorded with live cell imaging. The cap was selected as polygon ROI to gather intensity variation during the recovery process (yellow circle). The raw data matrix of the linearized FRAP ROI behavior over time is depicted in pseudo colors. **b.** Traditionally, intensities were averaged over time and fitted with single exponential fits.

Independent Source Separation

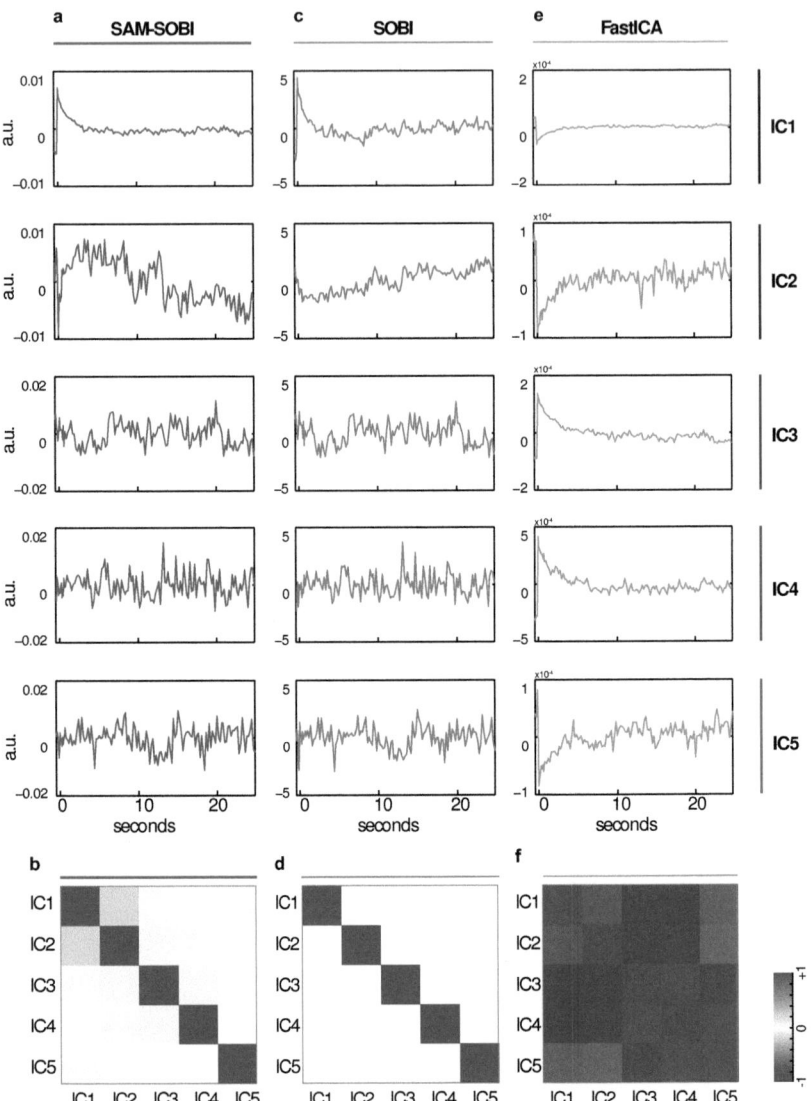

Figure 6.3: ICA of Cdc42P FRAP Experiment. Raw data of Cdc42 fused to GFP FRAP was analyzed by with three SAM-SOBI, SOBI and FastICA algorithms. Each five ICs were separated from the raw data by each algorithm (**a**, **c**, **e**, respectively). **b,d,f** depict correlation of respective IC source time series IC.

6.2 Manual FRAP Curve Fitting

protein mobilities, the algorithm SAM-SOBI was compared to SOBI (Belouchrani et al. 1993) and another ICA algorithm FastICA (Hyvarinen 1999). To extract the FRAP components from the Cdc42 ROI_{frap}, the three ICA algorithms were applied with their feature extraction option, thus, five source components were extracted from the raw dataset. The yielded independent components (ICs) were evaluated for the ability to de-mix signals, extract true Cdc42 mobilities in the polarity cap as well as noise robustness.

Cytome Feature Extraction with ICA

The extracted five IC (source signals) from the Cdc42 mobility experiments of the three ICA algorithms SAM-SOBI, SOBI and FastICA showed each a characteristic behavior (Figure 6.3). Most importantly, all three ICA algorithms were able to detect a FRAP-typical fluorescence recovery curve in their strongest IC (IC1). Note that IC values had arbitrary unit. To quantify the degree of IC similarity in time, pairwise correlation coefficients were calculated.

SAM-SOBI performed comparably well as SOBI with respect to signal demixing (Figure 6.3a). Interestingly, IC2 of SAM-SOBI recaptured a second FRAP-typical source signal as indicated by a measurable correlation of IC1 and IC2 (Figure 6.3b). Closer inspection of this second FRAP-typical curve revealed that the noisy signal had a lag phase of roughly ten second before the signal recovered close to the signal intensity prior to the FRAP event. In line with this indicator of a second potential protein mobility signal, Cdc42 was actually found to be recycled at the site of polarized growth via two independent recycling patterns (Slaughter et al. 2009, Freisinger unpublished). A cytosolic pathway was not only rapidly exchanging molecules in the cap, but also a slower actin-dependent pathway shuttled unbleached Cdc42

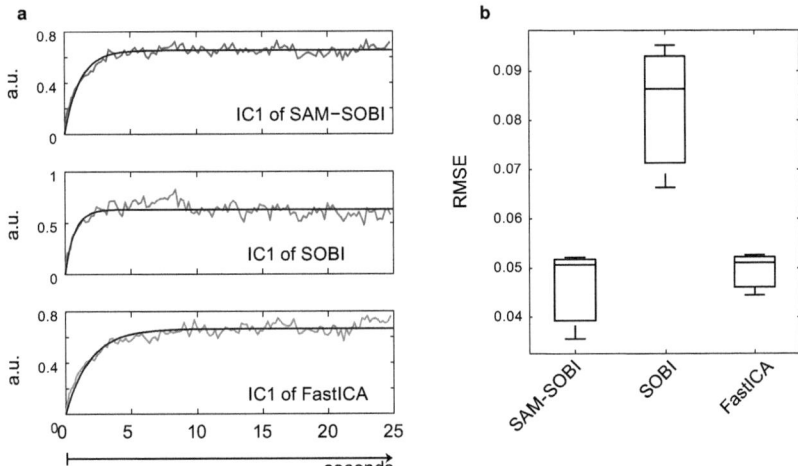

Figure 6.4: Biological evaluation of first independent components. b. IC1 of SAM-SOBI, SOBI and FastICA were fitted analogous to traditional FRAP analysis with a single exponential starting at timepoint 0. **c.** Root mean squared errors (RMSE) of IC1 of each three independent FRAP experiments judge the goodness of the exponential fit. Small errors to the fits indicate less noise in the IC.

6.2 Manual FRAP Curve Fitting

to the cap. The slower process may correspond to the FRAP curve in IC2 with the observed lag.

SOBI performed better than FastICA with respect to capture other independent components in IC2-5 beside the FRAP-typical curve in IC1 (Figure 6.3c). All IC were not correlated with one another (Figure 6.3d), indicating a successful signal de-mixing.

FastICA was not able to independently de-mix the FRAP data since the typical recovery was represented in all components (Figure 6.3e). As a result the supposably independent signals were still dependent (positively- or anti-correlated), subsequently not effectively de-mixed (Figure 6.3f). Note, that FastICA results were not deterministic, thus, another run of the algorithm may even yield one component that resembled a "noise component" (e.g. as shown in Theis et al. (2010)).

SAM-SOBI Noise-free Extraction of FRAP Curve

We elucidated the performance of IC1 in finding the true Cdc42 mobility value. The typical FRAP analysis included fitting of a single exponential to the recovery curve ($t \geq 0$, Figure 6.4a). We inverted and rescaled IC1 to (0,1) with respect to the basal value ($t = 0$) and pre-bleach values ($t < 0$). For noise-robust de-mixing algorithms we expected a precise fit.

Thus, we benchmarked the algorithms with the root mean squared error indicating the goodness of the fit. The measure of precision between IC values ($y_{ic}(t)$) and the curve at time t ($y_{fit}(t)$) was calculated over n timepoints like

$$\text{rmse} = \sqrt{\frac{(\sum_{t=0}^{n} y_{ic}(t) - y_{fit}(t))^2}{n}}$$

Overall, SAM-SOBI performed better than FastICA and SOBI, as their fit showed the smallest errors (Figure 6.4b). Small errors to the continuous noise-free fit function were therein an indicator of a noise-diminished component. We can conclude that SAM-SOBI did not only effectively determine IC but described source signals in a noise-robust manner.

6.3 Conclusion and Outlook

We did not only effectively couple an ICA algorithm to biological FRAP experiments but also demonstrated the superiority of a novel noise-robust ICA variant, called SAM-SOBI, over other ICA algorithms. The de-mixing of the underlying ICs of protein dynamics and substantial noise effects was best accomplished by SAM-SOBI. By employing protein dynamics of Cdc42 to benchmark the capabilities of SAM-SOBI, we were able to demonstrate that FRAP might be reliably analyzed with ICA and, thus, may replace the current manual analysis pipeline.

To further turn ICA variants into all-round tools to recover even more than one dynamic process from FRAP datasets, a variety of different experiments may be conducted. For example, individual regulator mechanisms of Cdc42 dynamics may be genetically manipulated *in vivo* and subsequently analyzed by FRAP with ICA. Furthermore, within the cap sub-spatial Cdc42 dynamics may even be revealed with a spatial ICA. But, first steps towards a robust FRAP analysis was already taken with our extensive analysis.

7 Outstanding Feature Detection

When experimentally measuring real datasets, unusual data points are nearly always present. Unusual data may be of various causes adding some sort of data distortion to the true or regular data points. Noise are usually unexplained random variations in the raw dataset. For example, technical noise generated by experimental instruments may have induced unwanted fluctuations. Outliers, in contrast, were outstanding data points numerically distant from the rest of the dataset. Following the definition of Hawkins (1980):

> "An outlier is an observation that deviates so much from other observations as to arouse suspicion that it was generated by a different mechanism."

Apparent from the definition of Hawkins outliers were always defined in the context of being "different" – assuming the remaining dataset to inhere some sort of "regularity". As a result, outlier definitions simultaneously imply a definition of the regular data – or the clusters. But, while most clustering algorithms did not separately handle outliers, outlier detection algorithms did not explicitly offer data clustering structures. In this context, we have developed the outlier detection algorithm CoCo that sampled for potential local cluster structures in order to get estimates and reliably identify all outliers in a dataset in an entirely automatic manner. Experimental validation was performed on a *peptidome* dataset.

Parts of this chapter were published: *CoCo* got published with equal contribution of Katrin Haegler in Böhm et al. (2009) and the peptidome dataset and filtering in Uwaje et al. (2007).

7.1 Biological Question and Data

7.1.1 Peptidome

Protein complexity continues to be a tremendous challenge for the analytical scientist. Shotgun mass spectrometry (MS) is the predominantly used method in high-throughput *proteomics* of complex protein mixtures. An essential component in shotgun *proteome* analyses is the use of high-resolution separation methodologies for the detection of a great number of the *peptidome* that made up these complex *proteome* mixtures.

Successful peptide identification with MS relies on the implementation of stringent criteria of a the peptide search algorithm. Even though optimal criteria are chosen false positive (FP) peptide hits may still occur. To that end, peptides may be separated prior to MS generating a validation criterion to improve the detection of those outstanding FP peptides.

The utilization of strips separating peptides by pH and subsequently focusing single peptides by their isoelectric point (pI) was a method that enabled the efficient separation of tryptic peptides (Essader et al. 2005). A pI is the pH at which a molecule (the peptide) has no net electrical charge (positive and negative charges are balanced). After peptide immobilization by pI, the strips were cut into pieces of regular sizes yielding information of an experimental pI of a peptide.

7.1.2 Peptidome Real Dataset Description

A standard proteomics set was used to generate the *peptidome* dataset. The enzymatically digested complex mixture was made up of 48 human proteins purified from either a natural source or recombinant bacteria. Peptides were separated on a strip by their pI on a pH gradient (3.5–4.5). The gradient strip was cut into pieces and subsequently measured and identified by MS (Uwaje et al. 2007).

The list of identified peptides were objects of the 2-dimensional raw dataset (Figure 7.1a). The first dimension was the information on the peptide's experimental pI determined simply by the position on the isoelectric strip. After peptide identification with MS the second dimension was induced by the theoretical pI calculated to validate the peptide hit. The theoretical pI was calculated from a peptide sequence which in turn was identified by the search algorithm after MS measurements. Wrong peptide identification yielded wrong sequences, thus, false theoretical pIs. FP peptides were those objects incorrectly identified. Consequently, these peptides are outstanding objects which require reliable detection.

7.2 Supervised Outlier Filtering

We first used a supervised filtering method to identify the FP in the raw *peptidome* dataset. Since outliers were considered to be generated by a different mechanism, the technical FP were considered to be outliers. The pIFilter approach (Uwaje et al. 2007) used a large amount of expert knowledge to filter the dataset in a supervised manner, whereas major steps included: Empirically determined threshold removed peptides with a low score from the search algorithm; Minimal peptide sequence length was assured; Position of the peptide on the IPG strip within a manually defined deviation around the mean strip pH was applied. The filtering steps with pIFilter identified 15 outliers (Figure 7.1b). The major drawback was, however, that only the expert knowledge enabled data analysis. Moreover, the visualization of the dataset itself did not give a valid reasoning why one peptide was consid-

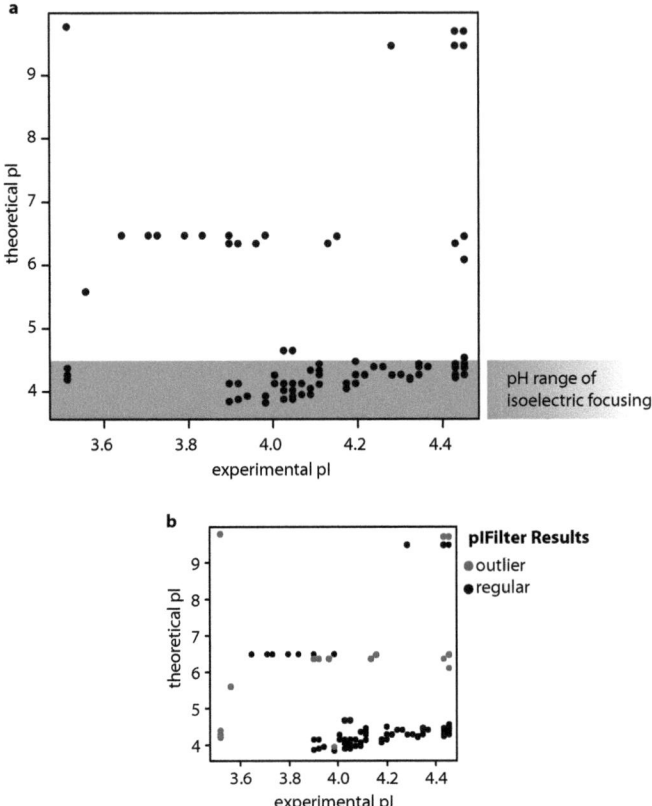

Figure 7.1: The standard *peptidome* measured by MS. a. The peptides were experimental separated by their pI and compared to their theoretical pI after identifying each peptide. Each data point was one peptide of one protein in the standard proteomics set. Green box indicated where peptides were expected to be distributed. Each data point was one peptide. **b.** Red data points were peptides identified to be outliers by pIFilter (Uwaje et al. 2007) while the remaining peptides supposably comprised the true regular dataset.

ered to be an outlier while others with similar coordinates were considered regular.

To improve outlier detection by avoiding any parametrization and without using any expert knowledge, an new outlier detection algorithm had to be developed.

7.3 Unsupervised Outlier Detection with CoCo

7.3.1 Introduction

Automatic outlier detection in large datasets is often equally or even more important than the detection of regularities. In various application fields like economy, biology, or medicine, the detection of extraordinary observations is of great interest. For example, the identification of criminal activities, such as credit card fraud, is crucial in electronic commerce applications (Knorr 1997). In biology, an automatic detection of outstanding measurements or noise is critical for high-throughput data generated with e.g. MS. The wide range of application fields also includes entertainment, sports, and many more.

Today, many data mining publications are in the field of clustering or outlier detection. The first field searches for regularities in a dataset whereby the second identifies irregular data. Closer consideration of both fields revealed a strong relationship, whereby one went barely without the other: On one hand, most clustering algorithms were confronted with outliers which deteriorated the cluster quality and/or destabilized the algorithm. Thus, all outliers should have been removed before clustering. On the other hand, outlier detection algorithms required a definition of the underlying cluster structure although clusters were not explicitly identified. Only if the cluster structure (of the regular data) is known, outliers are identified without any doubt. To formalize the outlier definition of Hawkins (1980) ordinary and potentially clustered points as well as outliers have to be differentiated with respect to a well-defined distinction criterion. In existing outlier detection approaches, the distinction criterion is a metric distance function together with parameter settings. The results are only meaningful if the distance function was well-characterized with respect to object similarities and suitable parameter settings. However, these premises assume a prior characterization of the dataset.

To cope with the problems of defining a distinct criterion and parametrization, we presented *CoCo*, a parameter-free outlier detection method based on the ideas of data compression and coding costs (Böhm et al. 2009). *CoCo* is able to identify all outliers in a data set based on a flexible definition of the regular data. The regular data is flexibly defined by a very general Probability Density Function (PDF), in our case a third-order mixture model of the Exponential Power Distribution (EPD). The EPD is a family of distribution functions which contained the Gaussian distribution, the uniform distribution, the Laplacian distribution, and a great variety of other distribution functions. Compared to previous outlier detection approaches, the EPD is not restricted to either uniform or Gaussian distribution functions. We demonstrate with our extensive benchmarking that the EPD was powerful enough to model the regular data in a variety of applications.

CoCo consideres a point P as outlier, unless nicely fitted in any of the distribution functions to be estimated within the neighborhood of P, independent of the neighborhood size. To measure the quality of the fit of P we adopt the idea of data compression: If a point fits well into a distribution function, it can be compressed efficiently. To connect the data compression efficiency of P with the degree of P being an outlier, the evaluation of the Minimum Description Length (MDL) principle is employed.

Outliers generated by a different mechanism may only be badly compressible while compression of regular objects was very strong. As a result the coding costs of a regular data point are much lower than those of out-

7.3 Unsupervised Outlier Detection with CoCo

liers. Inferred from the idea of Huffman coding, we apply the data compression idea by assigning few bits to frequent values and many bits to rare values. Frequent and rare values are clearly distinguished using the above mentioned EPD.

CoCo effectively applies the MDL principle to parameter-free outlier detection. No *a-priori* information about the dataset is required, like the number of clusters and outliers, the cluster size, a distance metric or the cluster density. Furthermore, we define a *CoCo* outlier factor with the concept of coding costs of an object, given the entire dataset. With the outlier factor we are able to clearly separate the cluster points from the outliers.

7.3.2 CoCo Bottom-Up Outlier Detection

With *CoCo*, we introduced an entirely parameter-free outlier detection method based on coding costs. Following Hawkins (1980), we adapted the outlier definition to the MDL principle for data compression. A data point was considered as outlier, if its compression rate was unusually high. As reference to define high compression rates, we consulted the compression rates of the cluster points. This approach nicely avoided the definition of a distance metric which would require thresholding of an undefined and unknown neighborhood.

Datasets may be rotated or distorted with respect to the Cartesian coordinate system. ICA enabled to process datasets which were not aligned to the orthogonal axes. However, the idea of an ordinary point had to be clearly defined. In contrast to currently available outlier detection methods, we expected experimental data to underlie not only Gaussian distributions. A generalization of the Gaussian PDF is the EPD. The EPD included, among several other distribution functions, the uniform, and the Laplacian PDF. By utilizing an EPD, no *a-priori* information on the type of distribution was required. Therefore, we generated no bias towards Gaussian data models. Combining ICA with EPD as the description of a regular subset of the dataset, we covered many real-world datasets without taking explicit care of cluster density, shape and orientation.

Entirely automatically, *CoCo* detected outliers having high coding costs with respect to the ordinary points which were effectively compressed. We implemented a bottom-up approach to identify all irregular data points while choosing the best compression model of ordinary points.

Algorithm 7.1 provides the CoCo pseudo-code. For each data point p, we initiated a set of nearest neighbors. Without prior knowledge of the underlying cluster shape, we extracted a substantial number of nearest neighbors nn_p based on their Euclidean distance to object p. We reliably de-mixed the set of nearest neighbors with ICA to ica_{nn_p} and fitted an EPD model epd_{nn_p}. Iteratively, we expanded the nearest neighbor set with those remaining data points to be best compressed based on the current epd_{nn_p}. After each update of the set of nearest neighbors nn_p, we adjusted the ica_{nn_p} and epd_{nn_p} since it was an expensive operation to estimate it anew. For each epd_{nn_p} estimate, we calculated the coding costs $cost_p$ of the object p under the given cluster description epd_{nn_p}. When the dataset was fully explored for each object p, we extracted the most suitable EPD cluster model by selecting the minimum compression rate of any object included in $costMinimum_{nn_p}$. The outlier factor for the data object $cost_p(j)$ was determined by its corresponding compression excess to $costMinimum_{nn_p}(j)$.

7.3.3 Regularity Estimates with CoCo

In the following, we defined the principles of ICA, EPD, data compression and linked them to the parameter-free outlier detection with *CoCo*.

Independent Component Analysis

It was observed that mixtures of signals were best de-mixed when searching for non-Gaussianity. Note, that the mixing of several source signals of ar-

7.3 Unsupervised Outlier Detection with CoCo

Algorithm 7.1 *CoCo*
---

input Database D

OF := {} # Outlier Factors

for data object $p \in D$ **do**
   cost_p := {}
   $\text{costMinimum}_{nn_p}$:= {}
   nn_p := initial set of nearest neighbors
   $\text{not\_}nn_p$:= $D \setminus nn_p$ # remaining points

   ica_{nn_p} := $ICA(nn_p)$
   $nn_{p,ica}$:= $\text{transform}(nn_p; ica_{nn_p})$
   epd_{nn_p} := estimate $EPD(nn_{p,ica})$
   while $\text{not\_}nn_p \neq \{\}$ **do**
     cost_p ∪= $\text{coding\_cost}(p_{ica}; epd_{nn_p})$
     $\text{costMinimum}_{nn_p}$ ∪= $\min(\text{coding\_cost}(nn_{p,ica}; epd_{nn_p}))$

     $\text{not\_}nn_{p,ica}$:= $\text{transform}(\text{not\_}nn_p; ica_{nn_p})$
     $\text{cost}_{\text{not\_}nn_{p,ica}}$:= $\text{coding\_cost}(\text{not\_}nn_{p,ica}; epd_{nn_p})$

     nn_p ∪= $\{\text{not\_}nn_{p,ica}$ with lowest $\text{cost}_{\text{not\_}nn_{p,ica}}\}$
     $\text{not\_}nn_p$:= $D \setminus nn_p$

     update ica_{nn_p}
     $nn_{p,ica}$:= $\text{transform}(nn_o; ica_{nn_p})$
     update epd_{nn_p}
   end while
   j := $\min(\text{costMinimum}_{nn_p})$ # index best compressed cluster
   $OF(p)$:= $(\text{cost}_p(j) - \text{costMinimum}_{nn_p}(j))$
end for

return $XMeans(OF)$ # to obtain outlier and cluster points

---

bitrary distribution types are always more Gaussian than the source signals themselves. The entropy of a Gaussian distribution was maximal, whereby, all other distributions had a lower entropy. Only minimization of the coding costs, measured by the entropy, guaranteed maximal compression efficiency. Thus, we applied the ICA to maximize non-Gaussianity as a measure of statistical independence. Its algorithm favored the directions in the data which were not similar to the Gaussian distribution.

We assumed that most datasets in experimental data usually did not follow equally dense distributions. They were rather distorted datasets with respect to the Cartesian coordinate system. The ICA first transformed the data into a so-called white space. Whitening involved de-correlation and normalization of the data to unit variance which enabled to implicitly handle unequally dense clusters.

Whitening may be performed with the Principal Component Analysis (PCA) that identified the directions of maximal variance $\vec{y}$, given a set of coordinates $\vec{x} \in C$ in a d-dimensional space. First, the data was centered $\vec{c} = \vec{x} - \vec{m}$ around the empirical mean

$$\vec{m} = \frac{1}{|C|} \sum_{\vec{x} \in C} \vec{x}$$

of the dataset C. Second, the centered data $\vec{c}$ had to be normalized to unit variance in all directions. The eigenvalue decomposition of the covariance matrix Σ is $\Sigma := V \times \Lambda \times V^T$, where V and Λ were orthogonal matrices containing the eigenvectors and eigenvalues of Σ, respectively. Finally, the PCA transformation of $\vec{x}$ was determined by

$$\vec{y} := \sqrt{\Lambda}^{-1} \times V^T \times \vec{c}.$$

Note, that $\Lambda = diag(\lambda_1, \ldots, \lambda_d)$ and $\sqrt{\Lambda}^{-1} = diag(\sqrt{1/\lambda_1}, \ldots, \sqrt{1/\lambda_d})$ were both diagonal matrices.

7.3 Unsupervised Outlier Detection with CoCo

For optimal projection of the data we next had to determine the directions of minimal entropy (determined with ICA) rather than the one of maximal variance (yielded by PCA). After transforming the data to white space, the FastICA algorithm (Hyvarinen 1999, Hyvärinen et al. 2001) determined a weighting matrix W containing the desired independent components (ICs). Regarding the original space, the ICs were not orthonormal in contrast to the principal components (PCs). The fix point iteration optimized $W = (\vec{w}_1, \ldots, \vec{w}_d)$, whereby the weight vectors were updated with the following rule:

$$\vec{w}_i := E\{\vec{y} \times g(\vec{w}_i^T \times \vec{y})\} - E\{g'(\vec{w}_i^T \times \vec{y})\} \times \vec{w}_i$$

We used $\tanh(s)$ for the non-linear contrast function $g(s)$. Note that $g'(s) = \frac{dg(s)}{ds}$ was the derivative of $g(s)$ and $E\{\ldots\}$ was the expected value. W was updated until convergence and then orthonormalized. The overall projection of the original data into the space of ICs was achieved by the de-mixing matrix M^{-1}. With $M = V \times \sqrt{\Lambda} \times W$ we denoted

$$M^{-1} = W^T \frac{1}{\sqrt{\Lambda}} V^T.$$

W and V were orthonormal matrices, thus the determinant was simply $det(M^{-1}) = \prod_{1 \leq i \leq d} \sqrt{1/\lambda_i}$. Recall that the rotation performed in the white space was expressed by W, and whitening was achieved by multiplying the coordinate vector by the scaled eigenvector matrix.

After the ICs were determined, we simply projected the data $\vec{x}$ into the IC space with

$$\vec{z} = M^{-1} \times (\vec{x} - \vec{m}).$$

Exponential Power Distribution

The EPD is a generalization of the Gaussian distribution in such a way, that it also included the Laplacian and the uniform distribution, depending on the parameter setting by exploiting the third-order statistics. Thus, its PDF has three different parameters to be fitted. Beside the location parameter μ, and the scale parameter σ, a shape parameter β is introduced (Mineo and Ruggieri 2005). For a random variable X, the EPD is defined as:

$$f_{EPD}(x;\mu,\sigma,\beta) = \frac{\exp(-\frac{|x-\mu|^\beta}{\beta\sigma^\beta})}{2\sigma\beta^{\frac{1}{\beta}}\Gamma(1+\frac{1}{\beta})}$$

Note that $\Gamma(s) = \int_0^\infty t^{s-1}\exp(-t)dt$ is the gamma function as an extension of the factorial operator for real numbers.

The shape parameter β determines kurtosis or the sharpness of the distribution. For $\beta > 2$, the EPD is platykurtic, with $\beta \to \infty$ mimicking a uniform distribution. For $\beta = 2$, the EPD corresponds to a Gaussian distribution. For $2 < \beta < 0$, the EPD is leptokurtic, including a Laplacian distribution for $\beta = 1$ (Figure 7.2a).

EPD after ICA

After projection of the coordinates into the white space and ICA, the data $\vec{z}$ was de-correlated and independent. This allowed to describe each dimension independently by an own EPD. Typically, a multi-dimensional data space contained d different PDF representations $f_{EPD}(z_i;\mu_i,\sigma_i,\beta_i)$ with $1 \leq i \leq d$. All d distributions were combined in a mixing matrix M, where the data points $\vec{x}$ corresponded to $\vec{x} = M \times \vec{z} + \vec{m}$, with $\vec{m}$ being the shifting vector and M determined by PCA, as described above. M allows the IC vectors to be not orthogonal. The EPD in a d-dimensional space (after ICA) was

7.3 Unsupervised Outlier Detection with CoCo

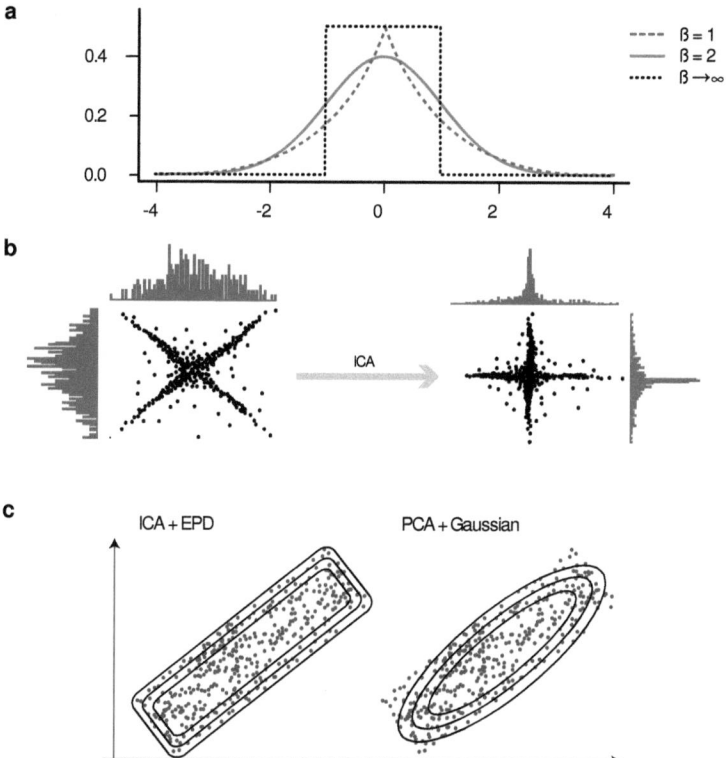

Figure 7.2: EPD coupled to ICA to Estimate Regularities. a. Different shapes of the EPD for different choices of parameter β. **b.** ICA generated redundancy in the data by centering, whitening and de-mixing. **c.** Dataset approximated with an EPD and a Gaussian distribution.

defined for a point $\vec{x}$ as

$$f_{EPD}(x; M^{-1}, \vec{m}, \mu, \sigma, \beta) = \frac{\prod_{1 \leq i \leq d} f_{EPD}(z_i; \mu_i, \sigma_i, \beta_i)}{|\det(M^{-1})|}$$

Figure 7.2c illustrates the effect of the approximation of a dataset with an EPD after ICA. The approximation of the same data with a Gaussian distribution (with PCA) would not achieve the same precision.

EPD Approximation

The estimation of the three parameters was a non-trivial problem. Although, $\mu_i = 0$ and $\sigma_i = 1$ were defined for $\beta = 2$ (Gaussian distribution) after ICA, μ_i and σ_i were no longer identical to the empirical mean and standard deviation, respectively. All three parameters μ_i, σ_i and β_i may be optimized by estimating the maximum likelihood, given a dataset C. Only a simultaneous approximation of all parameters ensured that the derivatives of the likelihood of the EPD vanished with respect to μ_i, σ_i and β_i.

Assuming μ_i and β_i to be given, the parameter σ_i was determined by differentiating the likelihood function with respect to σ_i of the EPD $\sum_{\vec{z} \in C} f_{EPD}(\vec{z}_i; \mu_i, \sigma_i, \beta_i)$:

$$\frac{d f_{EPD}(C; \mu_i, \sigma_i, \beta_i)}{d\sigma_i} = -\frac{|C|}{\sigma_i} + \frac{\sum_{\vec{z} \in C} |z_i - \mu_i|^{\beta_i}}{\sigma_i^{\beta_i+1}} = 0.$$

$$\Rightarrow \sigma_i = \left(\frac{1}{|C|} \sum_{\vec{z} \in C} |z_i - \mu_i|^{\frac{1}{\beta_i}} \right)$$

The parameters μ_i and β_i were to be optimized explicitly. We used a nested bisecting search as optimization technique to find β_i and μ_i in their parameter space. The direction to browse through the space was deter-

7.3 Unsupervised Outlier Detection with CoCo

mined by the derivatives of the log-likelihood function with respect to μ_i

$$\frac{d f_{EPD}(C; \mu_i, \sigma_i, \beta_i)}{d\mu_i} = -\frac{1}{\sigma_i^\beta} \sum_{\bar{z} \in C} |z_i - \mu_i|^{\beta_i - 1} \text{sign}(z_i - \mu_i)$$

and β_i

$$\frac{d f_{EPD}(C; \mu_i, \sigma_i, \beta_i)}{d\beta_i} = -\frac{|C|}{\beta_i^2}\left(\log \beta_i + \Psi\left(1 + \frac{1}{\beta_i}\right) - 1\right)$$
$$+ \frac{\sum_{\bar{z} \in C} s_i^{\beta_i} + \beta \log \sigma_i \sum_{\bar{z} \in C} s_i^{\beta_i} - \beta \sum_{\bar{z} \in C}(s_i^{\beta_i} - \log s_i)}{\beta_i^2 \sigma_i^{\beta_i}},$$

with $s_i = |z_i - \mu_i|$. $\Psi(s) = \frac{d \ln \Gamma(s)}{ds}$ was the digamma function being the logarithmic derivative of the gamma function. The EPD was estimated by this maximum likelihood approach until convergence of β_i.

7.3.4 Outlier Classification by Coding Costs

Coding Costs with MDL

After we estimated an exact representation $f_{EPD}(x; M^{-1}, \vec{m}, \mu, \sigma, \beta)$ of the data $\vec{x}$ with ICA and EPD, we designed a reliable approach to evaluate the accuracy of an object p to fit into f_{EPD}. We linked the concept of PDFs to the principle of data compression with the help of the MDL. Based on the Huffman coding, the number of bits required to transfer information on p were assigned with the inverse logarithm of the probability of the object. This negative log-likelihood represented the coding costs c_{PDF} of an object p with coordinates $\vec{x}$ given any PDF as:

$$c_{PDF}(\vec{x}) = \log_2\left(\frac{1}{f_{PDF}(\vec{x})}\right) = -\log_2(f_{PDF}(\vec{x})).$$

In order to represent the coding cost in the number of bits, the logarithm was typically used to a basis of 2. With *CoCo*, the EPD was used as PDF. Thus, the relative coding cost of a data point $\vec{x}$ under a given EPD after ICA was:

$$c_{EPD}(\vec{x}) = \log_2\left(|det(M^{-1})|\right) - \sum_{1 \le i \le d} \log_2\left(f_{EPD}(\vec{z}; \mu_i, \sigma_i, \beta_i)\right).$$

We did not to determine the absolute coding costs depending on different PDFs and the coding of the PDF parameters. It was absolutely crucial to determine statistically independent major directions with ICA to guarantee optimal data compression. Figure 7.2b shows that ICA transformed the data in such a way that it induced redundancy in the data with respect to the axes for best compression.

CoCo Outlier Factor and Detection

Putting everything together, for each set of coordinates $\vec{x}$ from the nearest neighbors nn_p generated with *CoCo*, we determined the rotation and the cluster description with EPD epd_{nn_p}. For each estimate epd_{nn_p}, the data compression rate was calculated with $c_{EPD}(\vec{p})$, $\vec{p}$ being the whitened coordinates of object p. We determined the efficiency to compress the data points nn_p, with an epd_{nn_p} estimate, with any object $q \in nn_p$ having minimal coding cost: We gathered information of compression rates for each set of nn_p with increasing size. Ideally we wanted to get the optimal neighborhood cluster size of p to determine the perfect compression of p regarding C. Practically, we only had information for each epd_{nn_p} estimated throughout the dataset. With it came the information of any object q exhibiting the minimal coding cost in the p neighborhood nn_p. The best compression rate $min(costMinimum_p)$ throughout all generated nn_p sets represented the best epd_{nn_p} estimate for any nn_p. In order to obtain the factor of p be-

7.3 Unsupervised Outlier Detection with CoCo

ing an outlier, the *CoCo* outlier factor was the absolute compression rate increase with respect to a minimal q.

The structure of a dataset was usually unknown. To that end, we screened C starting from p iteratively by adding a set of (nearest) neighbors; its size growing exponentially with respect to the size of C. To guarantee a stable estimate of EPD we initiated nn_p with a set of 20 neighbors. This screening approach of *CoCo* was however quadratic in the number of points n. In addition, the runtime was cubic in the dimensionality d due to PCA and EPD estimation.

After all *CoCo* outlier factors were obtained, we expected all outliers to exhibit unusually high costs in comparison to the ordinary, perhaps clustered points. The cluster points were compressed very effectively and showed outlier factors around 0. Flagging of outliers above a fixed threshold was difficult, since it would have involved to define a suitable threshold, which was a non-trivial task for an unknown dataset. Instead, we simply applied an X-Means algorithm to determine the set of clustering points being the cluster closest to 0. Theoretically, we may even establish an outlier order by simply organizing the other *CoCo* outlier factor groups in ascending order. In practice, X-Means usually found two clusters, one containing the clustering points, the other determining all outliers.

CoCo combined ICA with EPD as cluster description to determine outliers entirely parameter-free with the principle of data compression. No *a priori* knowledge of the number of outliers or the underlying cluster shape or density was required.

7.3.5 CoCo Benchmark Results

In the following we evaluated our outlier factor *CoCo* in comparison to LOF (Breunig et al. 2000) and LOCI (Papadimitriou et al. 2003) using one synthetic dataset as well as the *peptidome* dataset.

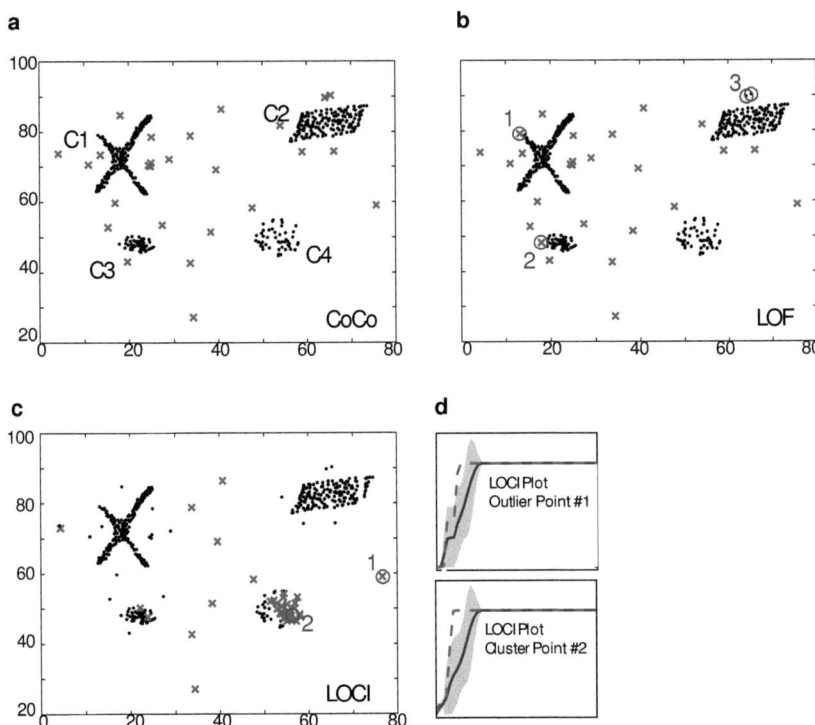

Figure 7.3: Outlier detection results from **a** *CoCo*, **b** LOF (MinPts = 50 selecting only the top 26 outliers), and **c** LOCI ($\alpha = 0.5$ and $r_{min} = 10$) for a synthetic dataset consisting of four clusters (C1-4) and 26 outliers. Detected outliers were highlighted with red crosses. **d** LOCI plot for two points detected as outliers. (1) True outlier. (2) Falsely labeled cluster point.

7.3 Unsupervised Outlier Detection with CoCo

Synthetic Data

We detected outliers of a synthetic dataset with our novel algorithm *CoCo* and compared them with outliers detected by LOF and LOCI. Figure 7.3a-c depict the results of *CoCo*, LOF, and LOCI for the synthetic dataset. The synthetic dataset consisted of four clusters C1-4 containing 184 (C1), 154 (C2), 52 (C3), and 50 (C4) data points. Each cluster had different cluster properties and a non-orthogonal major orientation. Cluster C3 underlay a Gaussian PDF. All together 26 outlier points not generated with any cluster distribution were added to the dataset.

CoCo correctly detected all 26 outlier points (Figure 7.3a). All belonged to one group of outliers, beside the group of cluster points shown in black. Note, that *CoCo* required not a single input parameter in order to identify all noise points. It handled different types of cluster shapes and orientations without expecting an explicit description of their distributions.

LOF was applied to identify the outliers based on a MinPts neighborhood of 50 determined by the size of the smallest cluster in the set (Figure 7.3b). We obtained the top 26 outliers since we knew how many outliers we generated for the present dataset. There were 24 out of the 26 noise points assigned correctly. Two noise points next to cluster C2 (Figure 7.3b, points circled in blue as No. 3) were not detected, leading to two falsely identified cluster points as outlier (Figure 7.3b, points circled in blue as No.1&2). Note, that we collected the top 26 data points ranked by the LOF score. Setting the parameter MinPts to a value smaller or equal than 10, LOF identified more cluster points as outliers while leaving many true outliers undetected (data not shown). MinPts values of 20 to 49 led to the same results as for 50, as presented here. If we had no *a priori* information on the number of outliers, it only would have been possible to determine an arbitrary number of outliers. In addition, an approximate cluster size needed to be known in advance to set MinPts, in order to get a meaningful output. These assumptions made it difficult to apply LOF to real world data.

LOCI was applied to our synthetic dataset with $\alpha = 0.5$ and $r_{min} = 10$ (Figure 7.3c) and identified 43 outlier points based on the suggested outlier flagging criteria. All together 17 true outliers were missed, while two points from within cluster C3 and 27 points from cluster C4 were labeled as outliers. Different parameter settings of r_{min} may detect more true outliers, but at the same time label more cluster points as outliers. Obviously, LOCI was not able to deal with low-density clusters, like C4. In Figure 7.3d, we had a closer look at the LOCI plot of an outlier point (Figure 7.3d, point circled in blue as No. 1) and a cluster point (No. 2). The LOCI plots looked very similar even though they were supposed to emphasize the difference between a cluster point and an outlier. Although we applied the algorithm with the suggested parameter settings, the result was difficult to interpret even after correspondence with the authors.

CoCo Outlier Factor Visualization

To emphasize the difference and strength of the *CoCo* outlier factor in comparison to the LOF score, we introduced a visualization of the "outlierness" (Figure 7.4). A scatter plot of the data in x-y directions was combined with a bar representation of the outlier factors in the z-dimension. We showed that the utilization of data compression was able to separate the outliers from the cluster points in comparison to the outlier factor of LOF. For the majority of the cluster points the *CoCo* coding costs were close to 0.0 indicated by short, dark blue bars. Outliers were either light blue or even red indicating their extraordinariness, ranging from 6.4 up to 24.2. Due to the

7.3 Unsupervised Outlier Detection with CoCo

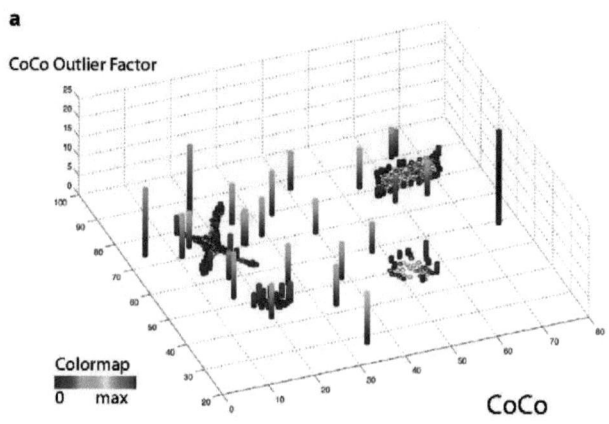

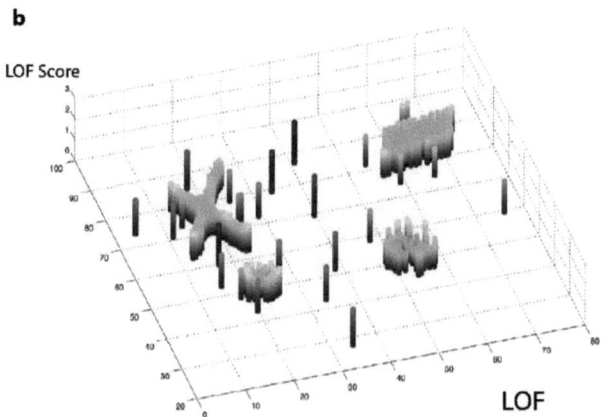

Figure 7.4: 3-dimensional Visualization of Outlier Factors. Outlier cost of *CoCo* (**a**) and outlier-factor of LOF (**b**) for the synthetic dataset in z-dimension.

large range between cluster points and outliers it was possible to clearly differentiate them using *CoCo*. In contrast, LOF produced almost continuous values ranging from 0.8 up to 2.3 which made it almost impossible to clearly differentiate cluster points from outliers explicitly.

The visualization of the outlier factors of LOF demonstrated, that the cluster structure was based on Euclidean distances: the outlier factors continuously increased circularly from the cluster centers to the cluster margins. In contrast to LOF, the *CoCo* outlier factors were equally low throughout an entire cluster except for the cluster edge points. It was based on the flexible cluster structure description using ICA and EPD.

Performance on Peptidome

CoCo was finally applied to the 2-dimensional *peptidome* dataset holding information on the experimental and the theoretic pI of peptides. In addition, LOF was applied, and the top-10 outliers manually selected as outliers (the number was determined by the number of outliers *CoCo* identified). LOCI was also applied but it yielded no outlier, not even with a less stringent cutoff of two deviations.

Outlier factors of *CoCo* and LOF were not identical (Figure 7.5). Considering the distribution of the outlier scores of *CoCo*, the outlier were clearly differentiable already by eye from regular data points. The ten outliers contained the most data points of extreme pIs above nine as well as a couple of single peptides where no similar experimental-to-theoretical pI values were measurable. In contrast, LOF was not able to clearly differentiate the outlier points from regular data points. Even more difficult for data analysis, the number of points to be considered outliers had to be manually set. We chose to select the same number of outliers as *CoCo* identified in a parameter-free manner. The outliers were now well distributed even in the experimentally valid and expected range (Figure 7.5 points inside green box). Several (clear) outlier points were identified by both the supervised filtering and *CoCo*, but

7.3 Unsupervised Outlier Detection with CoCo

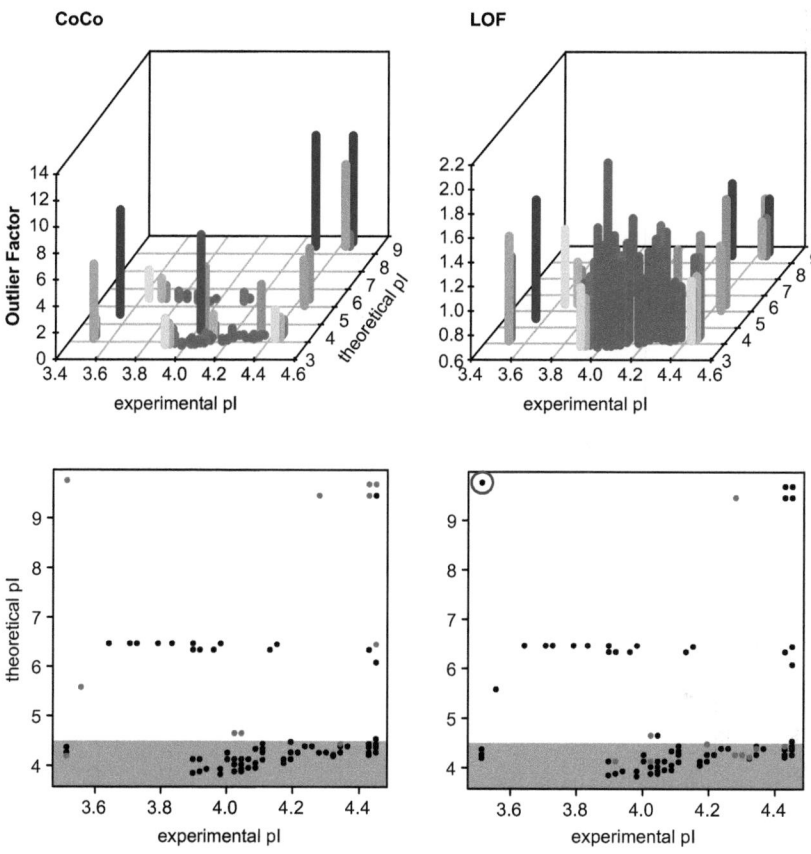

Figure 7.5: *CoCo* and LOF applied to standard *peptidome*. Outlier factors of *CoCo* and LOF were visualized in the z-dimension while the peptide data points were located along x-y axes. High values indicated factor for being an outlier. For *CoCo* all identified peptide outliers were marked in red, while the red marked peptides for LOF are the top-10 outliers.

were not detected with LOF (e.g. Figure 7.5 point circled). Even more severe, LOF failed to identify a single outlier marked as irregular by the supervised filtering. LOF and *CoCo* had three outliers in common, whereas *CoCo* and the supervised filtering shared six identified outlier points.

Compared to the supervised filtering set, *CoCo* was able to efficiently cope with the present dataset and yielded biologically comparable results. Unlike *CoCo*, LOF did not identify biologically reasonable outliers in the dataset of the *peptidome*.

7.4 Conclusion and Outlook

We have proposed *CoCo*, a parameter-free outlier detection. The perspective of data compression in outlier detection allowed to define a notion of outliers, which was intuitive to interpret and required no parameter settings. Our experiments demonstrated that *CoCo* was not restricted to Gaussian data but applicable to a wide range of data distributions.

In future work, we will further elaborate techniques to facilitate the interpretation of cost-based outliers. In addition, we may address the non-optimal runtime of *CoCo* which is hampered by the extensive screening of the neighborhoods. Clever heuristic to minimize the screening procedure together with e.g. object indexing strategies will allow to handle huge datasets.

8 Conclusion

The research projects on my doctoral dissertation was motivated by the broad spectrum of typical biological problems across major -*omics* fields. We solved the biological problems by not only developing novel but also advancing and improving current KDD solutions. To computationally retrieve the essential information from datasets produced by experimental methods, we successfully developed and advanced statistic and machine learning methods. The novel and intelligent algorithms developed allowed us to answer the posed biological questions across any molecular complexity level. Most methods developed yielded successful peer-review publications and were present on conferences.

8.1 Summary

Motivated by the challenge to be taken across biological fields, building blocks from statistics and machine learning were easily recycled to tackle their problems. Starting off with the versatile correlation coefficients, we were not only able to reveal rules which drive membrane protein segregation in the yeast plasma membrane (Chapter 5) but also to differentiate whether lipid correlations were specific with respect to effective perturbation of human Glioblastoma brain tumors (Chapter 4). Unlike the extraction of correlations in a dataset, a dataset de-correlation was necessary to separate underlying source signals, e.g. as for protein mobility measurements (Chapter 6). The noise-robust separation of independent components was therein most effective. By coupling the identification of independent components to the principle of data compression, we were able to reliably identify outstanding, false peptide identifications from arbitrarily distorted datasets (Chapter 7). When object similarities were only characterized by their linkage strength, we were able to recycle the data compression idea to find protein clusters enriched for biological functions (Chapter 3).

In general, the information retrieved from any type of dataset was determined what relationships objects have towards another. The detection of those objects most similar or even depend on each other may be equally important as the identification of those objects most dissimilar or even independent form each other. The strength of how object relate to each other has many facets. From objects tightly associated to substantially divergent, we dealt with: Objects in a graph sharing common features; Numeric objects so strongly related that their dependence was statistically assessable; On the contrary, numeric features underlying statistically independent components; And finally, objects outstanding in such a way that they had any information what so ever in common with the rest of the dataset. The type of KDD methods to be advanced or developed was chosen and designed to fit the desired objects relationships.

Ordered by object relationships towards another, the following paragraphs briefly summarize the individual research projects and their scientific achievements.

Chapter 3 comprises research projects on weighted graph clustering to find objects that share a general similarity. Motivated by the fact that the few available weighted graph clustering algorithms – even a global optimization heuristic with simulated annealing – failed to generate good and meaningful results for a yeast synthetic lethal *interactome*, we have developed a novel algorithm called *PaCCo*:

Nikola S. Müller, Katrin Haegler, Junming Shao, Claudia Plant and Christian Böhm. Weighted graph compression for parameter-free cluster-

8.1 Summary

ing with PaCCo. In *Proceedings of the 11th SIAM International Conference on Data Mining*, pages 932–43, 2011.

PaCCo coupled the principle of data compression via MDL to a two-way graph cluster definition constructed not only of high connectivity within one cluster but also an approximation of edge weight similarities. To practically find all clusters in a graph – without knowing how many clusters to derive – a bisecting k-means-inspired approach was implemented. During the entire process coding costs of the graph were constantly minimized and were additionally used as convergence criteria when bisecting was not further minimizing the overall coding costs. Benefits of the novel weighted graph clustering algorithm PaCCo over other algorithms were evaluated: First, PaCCo performed always better with more than 100 % additional noise edges. Second, PaCCo handled all weight distributions tested although the approximating function was only a Gaussian distribution, whereas some algorithm failed to cluster some distribution types. Third, runtime of the parameter-free PaCCo was almost as fast as a parameter-dependent algorithm and much faster than the other parameter-free algorithms. Finally, PaCCo detected clusters in the *interactome* which enriched more biological functions than any other clustering algorithm tested.

Chapter 4 searches for those lipid correlations that are differentially significant with respect to Glioblastoma. The Glioblastoma lipidome was experimentally measured for samples not affecting the immortality of these brain tumor cells and few samples successfully perturbing cells inducing the programmed cell death (apoptosis). To now detect only those correlations relevant to the sample of interest (SOI) – the one triggering apoptosis – we have developed an algorithm systematically revealing all partial correlations by a jackknife resampling approach:

Nikola S. Müller, Jan Krumsiek, Fabian J. Theis, Christian Böhm and Anke Meyer-Bäse. Gaussian graphical modeling reveals specific lipid correlations in glioblastoma cells. In *Proc. SPIE 8058, 805819 (2011)*, 2011.

Gaussian Graphical Models (GGM) were calculated by always leaving out one sample. The final differential GGM (*dGGM*) was then composed of the correlations which were either induced or suppressed by the SOI. We yielded a dGGM which subtracted out all unspecific correlations not relevant to the Glioblastoma lipidome. With the dGGM, we were able to pinpoint few individual lipids which potentially play more dominant roles in the apoptosis processes in the otherwise immortal Glioblastoma brain tumor cells.

Chapter 5 aims to reveal the principle of protein segregation in the yeast Plasma Membrane (PM) by examining the Image Pattern Dependencies. We derived new algorithms to process images in such a way that allowed us to infer principle of protein domain compositions:

> Felix Spira, Nikola S. Müller, Gisela Beck, Philipp von Olshausen, Joachim Beig and Roland Wedlich-Soldner. Patchwork organization of the yeast plasma membrane into numerous coexisting domains. *Nature Cell Biology*, 14(6):640–648, 2012.

> Nikola S. Müller, Roland Wedlich-Soldner and Felix Spira. From mosaic to patchwork: matching lipids and proteins in membrane organization. *Mol. Membr. Biol.*, 29(5):186–196, 2012.

Both, the new microscopy technique and the preliminary biological results, gave reasons to develop novel image processing algorithm not yet available. We quantified lateral protein distributions on the PM by a novel algorithm which used solely one-color microscopy images and converted the observed patterns into one factor. The resulting network factor is based on integration of histogram curves and successfully recapitulated the numerous similar but still different patterns ranging between patch- and network-like distribution types. Ultimately, the domain compositions of the yeast PM was assessed via extensive image correlation methods of two-color microscopy. Computationally generating cells determined our expected random domain colo-

8.1 Summary

calization values. By pairwise correlation of entire dataset we revealed that protein domain formation largely affects domain overlaps. Consequently domain overlap itself has a random nature – except of active segregation of a few domains. The new image processing algorithms helped to advance understanding of PM protein domain formation. Whereas, false biological conclusion would have been drawn when not analyzed with our algorithms.

Chapter 6 elucidates the potential of Independent Source Separation techniques. To measure protein mobilities, microscopy of cytomes in combination with a noise-robust variant of the independent component analysis (ICA) was proven to be highly effective. The ICA algorithm capable of separating protein mobility sources from noise components in yeast cytome was published in:

> Fabian J. Theis, Nikola S. Müller, Claudia Plant and Christian Böhm. Robust second-order source separation identifies experimental responses in biomedical imaging. In *Proceedings of the 9th international conference on Latent variable analysis and signal separation*, pages 466–73, 1929209, 2010. Springer-Verlag.

The SAM-SOBI implementation was shown to separate independent noise sources form the time-lapse microscopy images while revealing one typical curve of which protein mobility is inferred. Interestingly, only SAM-SOBI was able to detect a second, although more noisy, independent component capturing the second population of slower protein mobility. The analysis of the experimental procedure to infer protein mobilities with the noise-robust SAM-SOBI was demonstrated to be able to replace a careful, manual analysis workflow.

Chapter 7 describes a novel algorithm to automatically find Outstanding Feature Detection. The unsupervised detection of falsely identified peptides is crucial to infer correct protein information. We developed a novel and entirely automatic outlier detection algorithm called *CoCo*, which was able to detect all peptidome outliers and outcompete other outlier detection algorithms. We implemented *CoCo* to detect all outliers by exploiting the principle of data compression:

> Christian Böhm, Katrin Haegler, Nikola S. Müller and Claudia Plant. CoCo: coding cost for parameter-free outlier detection. In *Proceedings of the 15th ACM SIGKDD international conference on Knowledge discovery and data mining*, pages 149–58, 1557042, 2009. ACM.

We scanned the neighborhoods of each object in the dataset and tried to place the object into a potential cluster structure. The potential clusters capture the regularity in the dataset and was assumed to be of arbitrary shape and distribution. The combination of ICA with a third-order probability density function allowed us to detect outliers close to rotated and sheared clusters. We coupled data compression into the algorithm *CoCo* to evaluate whether an object fits well into a potential cluster in its neighborhood. Resulting coding costs of each object allowed an obvious differentiation of outliers and regular data points.

8.2 Future Directions

Beyond the algorithms developed during my doctoral work several ideas may help to further advance KDD analyses of *-omics* data. The individually proposed algorithms may each be improved by further addressing the algorithmic details. For example, logically coupling node linkage with node weight information to improve *PaCCo*, mathematically solving a *dGGM* circumventing the resampling strategy, using partial correlation analyses to reveal biological segregation mechanism of *membrane proteome*, applying a spatial ICA to get information on local hotspots of increased protein mobility as well as replacing neighborhood screening in *CoCo* to speed up runtime.

In addition, highly valuable may be the combination of algorithms across KDD techniques. For example, simultaneously detecting outliers and find-

8.2 Future Directions

ing clusters in graphs by data compression will allow a more integrative data analysis – especially helpful for *-omics* problems to infer globally correct information (e.g. cluster node or outlier) on individual molecular objects. Moreover, statistical dependence and independence analyses joined in a KDD approach might help to find those components separating some source information from those where information is not separable – instead of forcing separation or correlation of the entire dataset. The biological integration of two or more *-omics* datasets will require the development of algorithms handling mixed datasets. For example, graphs with additional numeric information of nodes may be incorporated into *PaCCo* by extending the compression function. With those correlation and independence algorithms, we have developed for major *-omics* datasets, we offer several promising new staring points for future projects.

A References

D. Abhimanyu and K. David. Algorithms for subset selection in linear regression. In *Proceedings of the 40th annual ACM symposium on Theory of computing*, STOC '08l, pages 45–54. ACM, 2008.

R. G. Anderson and K. Jacobson. A role for lipid shells in targeting proteins to caveolae, rafts, and other lipid domains. *Science*, 296(5574):1821–5, 2002.

S. Ando and R. K. Yu. Fatty acid and long-chain base composition of gangliosides isolated from adult human brain. *Journal of Neuroscience Research*, 12(2-3):205–11, 1984.

B. Andreopoulos, A. An, X. Wang, and M. Schroeder. A roadmap of clustering algorithms: finding a match for a biomedical application. *Brief Bioinform*, 10(3):297–314, 2009.

M. Ashburner, C. A. Ball, J. A. Blake, D. Botstein, H. Butler, J. M. Cherry, A. P. Davis, K. Dolinski, and et al. Gene ontology: tool for the unification of biology. the gene ontology consortium. *Nature Genetics*, 25:25–9, 2000.

D. Axelrod, N. L. Thompson, and T. P. Burghardt. Total internal inflection fluorescent microscopy. *Journal of microscopy*, 129(Pt 1):19–28, 1983.

L. A. Bagatolli, J. H. Ipsen, A. C. Simonsen, and O. G. Mouritsen. An outlook on organization of lipids in membranes: Searching for a realistic connection with the organization of biological membranes. *Prog Lipid Res*, 2010.

A. L. Barabasi and Z. N. Oltvai. Network biology: understanding the cell's functional organization. *Nat Rev Genet*, 5(2):101–13, 2004.

A. Barron, J. Rissanen, and B. Yu. The minimum description length principle in coding and modeling. *IEEE Transactions on Information Theory*, 44(6):2743–60, 1998.

A. Belouchrani, K. Abed-meraim, J. F. Cardoso, and E. Moulines. Second order blind separation of temporally correlated sources, 1993.

D. Berchtold and T. C. Walther. Torc2 plasma membrane localization is essential for cell viability and restricted to a distinct domain. *Mol Biol Cell*, 20(5):1565–75, 2009.

M. W. Berry, S. T. Dumais, and G. W. O'Brien. Using linear algebra for intelligent information retrieval. *Siam Review*, 37(4):573–95, 1995.

A. Beyer, S. Bandyopadhyay, and T. Ideker. Integrating physical and genetic maps: from genomes to interaction networks. *Nature reviews. Genetics*, 8(9):699–710, 2007.

H. Bing, X. Fengong, Z. Xiaoyu, Z. Jian, and G. Wei. Exo70 interacts with phospholipids and mediates the targeting of the exocyst to the plasma membrane. *EMBO J*, 26(18):4053–65, 2007.

C. Boone, H. Bussey, and B. J. Andrews. Exploring genetic interactions and networks with yeast. *Nat Rev Genet*, 8(6):437–49, 2007.

E. I. Boyle, S. Weng, J. Gollub, H. Jin, D. Botstein, J. M. Cherry, and G. Sherlock. Go::termfinder–open source software for accessing gene ontology information and finding significantly enriched gene ontology terms associated with a list of genes. *Bioinformatics*, 20(18):3710–5, 2004.

M. M. Breunig, H-P. Kriegel, R. T. Ng, and J. Sander. Lof: Identifying density-based local outliers. In *SIGMOD Conference*, pages 93–104, 2000.

S. Brohee and J. van Helden. Evaluation of clustering algorithms for protein-protein interaction networks. *BMC Bioinformatics*, 7:488, 2006.

S. Brohee, K. Faust, G. Lima-Mendez, G. Vanderstocken, and J. van Helden. Network analysis tools: from biological networks to clusters and pathways. *Nat Protoc*, 3(10):1616–29, 2008.

D. Bu, Y. Zhao, L. Cai, H. Xue, X. Zhu, H. Lu, J. Zhang, S. Sun, and et al. Topological structure analysis of the protein-protein interaction network in budding yeast. *Nucleic Acids Res*, 31(9):2443–50, 2003.

A. J. Butte, P. Tamayo, D. Slonim, T. R. Golub, and I. S. Kohane. Discovering functional relationships between rna expression and chemotherapeutic susceptibility using relevance networks. *Proc Natl Acad Sci U S A*, 97(22): 12182–6, 2000.

C. Böhm, C. Faloutsos, J-Y. Pan, and C. Plant. Robust information-theoretic clustering. In *Proceedings of the 12th ACM SIGKDD international conference on Knowledge discovery and data mining*, pages 65–75, 1150414, 2006. ACM.

C. Böhm, C. Faloutsos, and C. Plant. Outlier-robust clustering using independent components. In *Proceedings of the 2008 ACM SIGMOD international conference on Management of data*, pages 185–98, 1376638, 2008. ACM.

C. Böhm, K. Haegler, N. S. Mueller, and C. Plant. Coco: coding cost for parameter-free outlier detection. In *Proceedings of the 15th ACM SIGKDD international conference on Knowledge discovery and data mining*, pages 149–58, 1557042, 2009. ACM.

G. W. Carter, D. J. Galas, and T. Galitski. Maximal extraction of biological information from genetic interaction data. *PLoS Comput Biol*, 5(4): e1000347, 2009.

Appendix References

V. Cerny. Thermodynamical approach to the traveling salesman problem: An efficient simulation algorithm. *Journal of Optimization Theory and Applications*, 45(1):41–51, 1985.

S. Charrin, F. le Naour, O. Silvie, P. E. Milhiet, C. Boucheix, and E. Rubinstein. Lateral organization of membrane proteins: tetraspanins spin their web. *Biochem J*, 420(2):133–54, 2009.

Y. R. Cho, W. Hwang, M. Ramanathan, and A. Zhang. Semantic integration to identify overlapping functional modules in protein interaction networks. *BMC Bioinformatics*, 8:265, 2007.

S. R. Collins, P. Kemmeren, X. C. Zhao, J. F. Greenblatt, F. Spencer, F. C. Holstege, J. S. Weissman, and N. J. Krogan. Toward a comprehensive atlas of the physical interactome of saccharomyces cerevisiae. *Mol Cell Proteomics*, 6(3):439–50, 2007.

P. Comon. Independent component analysis, a new concept. *Signal Processing*, 36(3):287–314, 1994.

U. Coskun and K. Simons. Membrane rafting: From apical sorting to phase segregation. *FEBS Lett*, 2009.

M. Costanzo, A. Baryshnikova, J. Bellay, Y. Kim, E. D. Spear, C. S. Sevier, H. Ding, J. L. Koh, and et al. The genetic landscape of a cell. *Science*, 327 (5964):425–31, 2010.

L. Danon, A. az Guilera, J. Duch, and A. Arenas. Comparing community structure identification. *Journal of Statistical Mechanics: Theory and Experiment*, 2005(09):P09008–P, 2005.

A. de la Fuente, N. Bing, I. Hoeschele, and P. Mendes. Discovery of meaningful associations in genomic data using partial correlation coefficients. *Bioinformatics*, 20(18):3565–74, 2004.

C. Deepayan, P. Spiros, M. S. Dharmendra, and F. Christos. Fully automatic cross-associations. In *KDD '04: Proceedings of the tenth ACM SIGKDD international conference on Knowledge discovery and data mining*, pages 79–88, 2004.

A. D. Douglass and R. D. Vale. Single-molecule microscopy reveals plasma membrane microdomains created by protein-protein networks that exclude or trap signaling molecules in t cells. *Cell*, 121(6):937–50, 2005.

C. S. Ejsing, J. L. Sampaio, V. Surendranath, E. Duchoslav, K. Ekroos, R. W. Klemm, K. Simons, and A. Shevchenko. Global analysis of the yeast lipidome by quantitative shotgun mass spectrometry. *Proceedings of the National Academy of Sciences of the United States of America*, 106(7):2136–41, 2009.

A. S. Essader, B. J. Cargile, J. L. Bundy, and Jr. Stephenson, J. L. A comparison of immobilized ph gradient isoelectric focusing and strong-cation-exchange chromatography as a first dimension in shotgun proteomics. *Proteomics*, 5(1):24–34, 2005.

S. Fortunato. Community detection in graphs. *Physics Reports*, 486(3-5): 75–174, 2010.

A. C. Gavin, M. Bosche, R. Krause, P. Grandi, M. Marzioch, A. Bauer, J. Schultz, J. M. Rick, and et al. Functional organization of the yeast proteome by systematic analysis of protein complexes. *Nature*, 415(6868): 141–7, 2002.

M. Girvan and M. E. J. Newman. Community structure in social and biological networks. *Proceedings of the National Academy of Sciences of the United States of America*, 99(12):7821–6, 2002.

P. Gormanns, N. S. Mueller, C. Ditzen, S. Wolf, F. Holsboer, and C. W. Turck. Phenome-transcriptome correlation unravels anxiety and depression related pathways. *Journal of psychiatric research*, 45(7):973–9, 2011.

R. Guimera and L. A. Nunes Amaral. Functional cartography of complex metabolic networks. *Nature*, 433(7028):895–900, 2005.

R. Guimera, M. Sales-Pardo, and L. A. Amaral. Modularity from fluctuations in random graphs and complex networks. *Physical review. E, Statistical, nonlinear, and soft matter physics*, 70(2 Pt 2):025101, 2004.

U. Guldener, M. Munsterkotter, M. Oesterheld, P. Pagel, A. Ruepp, H. W. Mewes, and V. Stumpflen. Mpact: the mips protein interaction resource on yeast. *Nucleic Acids Res*, 34(Database issue):D436–41, 2006.

R. Görke, A. Meyer-Bäse, D. Wagner, H. He, M. R. Emmett, and C. A. Conrad. Determining and interpreting correlations in lipidomic networks found in glioblastoma cells. *BMC Syst Biol*, 4:126, 2010.

R. Harkewicz and E. A. Dennis. Applications of mass spectrometry to lipids and membranes. *Annual Review of Biochemistry*, 2010.

D. Hawkins. *Identification of Outliers*. Chapman and Hall, London, 1980.

H. He, C. L. Nilsson, M. R. Emmett, Y. Ji, A. G. Marshall, R. A. Kroes, J. R. Moskal, H. Colman, and et al. Polar lipid remodeling and increased sulfatide expression are associated with the glioma therapeutic candidates, wild type p53 elevation and the topoisomerase-1 inhibitor, irinotecan. *Glycoconjugate Journal*, 27(1):27–38, 2010.

D. J. Higham, M. Rasajski, and N. Przulj. Fitting a geometric graph to a protein-protein interaction network. *Bioinformatics*, 24(8):1093–9, 2008.

P. Holme and M. Huss. Role-similarity based functional prediction in networked systems: application to the yeast proteome. *J R Soc Interface*, 2 (4):327–33, 2005.

W. Hwang, Y. R. Cho, A. Zhang, and M. Ramanathan. A novel functional module detection algorithm for protein-protein interaction networks. *Algorithms Mol Biol*, 1:24, 2006.

A. Hyvarinen. Fast and robust fixed-point algorithms for independent component analysis. *IEEE Transactions on Neural Networks*, 10(3):626–34, 1999.

A. Hyvärinen, J. Karhunen, and E. Oja. *Independent Component Analysis*. 2001.

M. I. Jordan and F. R. Bach. Learning spectral clustering. In *Advances in Neural Information Processing Systems 16*, 2003.

M. Kanehisa, S. Goto, M. Furumichi, M. Tanabe, and M. Hirakawa. Kegg for representation and analysis of molecular networks involving diseases and drugs. *Nucleic Acids Research*, 38(Database issue):D355–60, 2010.

G. Karypis and V. Kumar. Metis: A software package for partitioning unstructured graphs, partitioning meshes, and computing fill-reducing orderings of sparse matrices. version 4.0. Technical report, Dept. of Computer Science, University of Minnesota, 1998a.

G. Karypis and V. Kumar. A fast and high quality multilevel scheme for partitioning irregular graphs. *SIAM Journal on Scientific Computing*, 20: 359–92, 1998b.

G. Karypis and V. Kumar. Multilevel k-way partitioning scheme for irregular graphs. *Journal of Parallel and Distributed Computing*, 48:96 – 129, 1998c.

E. Keogh, S. Lonardi, and C. A. Ratanamahatana. Towards parameter-free data mining. In *KDD '04: Proceedings of the tenth ACM SIGKDD international conference on Knowledge discovery and data mining*, pages 206–15. ACM, 2004.

S. Kim and I-S. Kweon. Simultaneous classification and visualword selection using entropy-based minimum description length. In *ICPR (1)*, pages 650–3, 2006.

S. Kirkpatrick, Jr. Gelatt, C. D., and M. P. Vecchi. Optimization by simulated annealing. *Science*, 220(4598):671–80, 1983.

E. M. Knorr. On digital money and card technologies. Technical Report Technical Report 97-02, University of British Columbia, 1997.

E. M. Knorr and R. T. Ng. A unified notion of outliers: Properties and computation. In *KDD*, pages 219–22, 1997.

E. M. Knorr and R. T. Ng. Algorithms for mining distance-based outliers in large datasets. In *VLDB*, pages 392–403, 1998.

E. M. Knorr and R. T. Ng. Finding intensional knowledge of distance-based outliers. In *VLDB*, pages 211–22, 1999.

J. Krumsiek, K. Suhre, T. Illig, J. Adamski, and F. J. Theis. Gaussian graphical modeling reconstructs pathway reactions from high-throughput metabolomics data. *BMC Syst Biol*, 5(1):21, 2011.

A. Kusumi, Y. Sako, and M. Yamamoto. Confined lateral diffusion of membrane receptors as studied by single particle tracking (nanovid microscopy). effects of calcium-induced differentiation in cultured epithelial cells. *Biophys J*, 65(5):2021–40, 1993.

D. Lingwood, H.-J. Kaiser, I. Levental, and K. Simons. Lipid rafts as functional heterogeneity in cell membranes. *Biochem Soc Trans*, 37(Pt 5):955–60, 2009.

S. Lloyd. Least squares quantization in pcm. *Information Theory, IEEE Transactions on*, 28(2):129–37, 1982.

M. Loibl, G. Grossmann, V. Stradalova, A. Klingl, R. Rachel, W. Tanner, J. Malinsky, and M. Opekarova. C terminus of nce102 determines the structure and function of microdomains in the saccharomyces cerevisiae plasma membrane. *Eukaryotic cell*, 9(8):1184–92, 2010.

F. Luo, Y. Yang, C. F. Chen, R. Chang, J. Zhou, and R. H. Scheuermann. Modular organization of protein interaction networks. *Bioinformatics*, 23(2):207–14, 2007.

J. B. Macqueen. Some methods of classification and analysis of multivariate observations. In *Proceedings of the Fifth Berkeley Symposium on Mathematical Statistics and Probability*, pages 281–97, 1967.

P. M. Magwene and J. Kim. Estimating genomic coexpression networks using first-order conditional independence. *Genome Biol*, 5(12):R100, 2004.

K. Malínská, J. Malínská, M. Opekarová, and W. Tanner. Visualization of protein compartmentation within the plasma membrane of living yeast cells. *Mol Biol Cell*, 14(11):4427–36, 2003.

K. Malínská, J. Malínsky, M. Opekarova, and W. Tanner. Distribution of can1p into stable domains reflects lateral protein segregation within the plasma membrane of living s. cerevisiae cells. *J Cell Sci*, 117(Pt 25):6031–41, 2004.

E. M. M. Manders, F. J. Verbeek, and J. A. Aten. Measurement of co-localization of objects in dual-colour confocal images. *Journal of Microscopy (Oxford)*, 169:375–82, 1993.

R. G. Miller. The jackknife-a review. *Biometrika*, 61(1):1–15, 1974.

A. Mineo and M. Ruggieri. A software tool for the exponential power distribution: The normalp package. *Journal of Statistical Software*, 12(4), 2005.

A. A. Monakov. Estimation of the covariance matrix for dependent signal samples: polarization diversity systems. *IEEE J AES*, 30(2):484–92, 1994.

O. G. Mouritsen and M. Bloom. Models of lipid-protein interactions in membranes. *Annu Rev Biophys Biomol Struct*, 22:145–71, 1993.

N. S. Mueller, R. Wedlich-Soldner, and F. Spira. From mosaic to patchwork: matching lipids and proteins in membrane organization. *Mol. Membr. Biol.*, 29(5):186–196, Aug 2012.

J. Mulholland, D. Preuss, A. Moon, A. Wong, D. Drubin, and D. Botstein. Ultrastructure of the yeast actin cytoskeleton and its association with the plasma membrane. *The Journal of cell biology*, 125(2):381–91, 1994.

N. S. Müller, K. Haegler, J. Shao, C. Plant, and C. Böhm. Weighted graph compression for parameter-free clustering with pacco. In *Proceedings of the 11th SIAM International Conference on Data Mining*, pages 932–43, 2011a.

N. S. Müller, J. Krumsiek, F. J. Theis, C. Böhm, and A. Meyer-Bäse. Gaussian graphical modeling reveals specific lipid correlations in glioblastoma cells. In *Proc. SPIE 8058, 805819 (2011)*, 2011b.

M. E. Newman. Modularity and community structure in networks. *Proc Natl Acad Sci U S A*, 103(23):8577–82, 2006.

M. E. Newman and M. Girvan. Finding and evaluating community structure in networks. *Phys Rev E Stat Nonlin Soft Matter Phys*, 69(2 Pt 2): 026113, 2004.

A. Y. Ng, M. I. Jordan, and Y. Weiss. On spectral clustering: Analysis and an algorithm. In *Advances in Neural Information Processing Systems 14*, pages 849 – 56, 2001.

R. Opgen-Rhein and K. Strimmer. Using regularized dynamic correlation to infer gene dependency networks from time-series microarray data. pages 73–6, 2006.

R. Opgen-Rhein and K. Strimmer. From correlation to causation networks: a simple approximate learning algorithm and its application to high-dimensional plant gene expression data. *BMC Syst Biol*, 1:37, 2007.

S. Papadimitriou, H. Kitagawa, P. B. Gibbons, and C. Faloutsos. Loci: Fast outlier detection using the local correlation integral. In *ICDE*, pages 315–, 2003.

D. Pelleg and A. W. Moore. X-means: Extending k-means with efficient estimation of the number of clusters. In *ICML '00: Proceedings of the Seventeenth International Conference on Machine Learning*, pages 727–34, 2000.

S. Pinkert, J. Schultz, and J. Reichardt. Protein interaction networks–more than mere modules. *PLoS Computational Biology*, 6(1):e1000659, 2010.

M. Puchades, C. L Nilsson, M. R. Emmett, K. D. Aldape, Y. Ji, F. F. Lang, T-J. Liu, and C. A. Conrad. Proteomic investigation of glioblastoma cell lines treated with wild-type p53 and cytotoxic chemotherapy demonstrates an association between galectin-1 and p53 expression. *J Proteome Res*, 6(2): 869–75, 2007.

J. Rissanen. A universal prior for integers and estimation by minimum description length. *The Annals of Statistics*, 11(2):416–31, 1983.

J. Rissanen. Mdl denoising. *IEEE Transactions on Information Theory*, 46(7):2537–43, 2000.

M. Robnik-Sikonja and I. Kononenko. Pruning regression trees with mdl. In *ECAI*, pages 455–9, 1998.

E. Sackmann, R. Lipowsky, and E. Sackmann. *Chapter 1 Biological membranes architecture and function*, volume 1, part 1, pages 1–63. North-Holland, 1995.

S. Schaeffer. Graph clustering. *Computer Science Review*, 1(1):27–64, 2007.

M. Schuldiner, S. R. Collins, N. J. Thompson, V. Denic, A. Bhamidipati, T. Punna, J. Ihmels, B. Andrews, and et al. Exploration of the function and organization of the yeast early secretory pathway through an epistatic miniarray profile. *Cell*, 123(3):507–19, 2005.

M. Schuldiner, S. R. Collins, J. S. Weissman, and N. J. Krogan. Quantitative genetic analysis in saccharomyces cerevisiae using epistatic miniarray profiles (e-maps) and its application to chromatin functions. *Methods*, 40(4):344–52, 2006.

J. Schäfer and K. Strimmer. Learning large-scale graphical gaussian models from genomic data. In *In Science of Complex Networks: From Biology to the Internet and WWW*, 2005a.

J. Schäfer and K. Strimmer. A shrinkage approach to large-scale covariance matrix estimation and implications for functional genomics. *Stat Appl Genet Mol Biol*, 4:Article32, 2005b.

C. E. Shannon. A mathematical theory of communication. *Bell System Technical Journal*, 27(4):623–56, 1948.

K. Simons and E. Ikonen. Functional rafts in cell membranes. *Nature*, 387 (6633):569–72, 1997.

S. J. Singer and G. L. Nicolson. The fluid mosaic model of the structure of cell membranes. *Science*, 175(23):720–31, 1972.

B. D. Slaughter, A. Das, J. W. Schwartz, B. Rubinstein, and R. Li. Dual modes of cdc42 recycling fine-tune polarized morphogenesis. *Developmental Cell*, 17(6):823–35, 2009.

E. L. Snapp, N. Altan, and J. Lippincott-Schwartz. Measuring protein mobility by photobleaching gfp chimeras in living cells. *Current protocols in cell biology*, Chapter 21:Unit 21 1, 2003.

J. Song and M. Singh. How and when should interactome-derived clusters be used to predict functional modules and protein function? *Bioinformatics*, 25(23):3143–50, 2009.

I. A. Sparkes, K. Graumann, A. Martiniere, J. Schoberer, P. Wang, and A. Osterrieder. Bleach it, switch it, bounce it, pull it: using lasers to reveal plant cell dynamics. *Journal of Experimental Botany*, 62(1):1–7, 2011.

F. Spira, N. S. Mueller, G. Beck, P. von Olshausen, J. Beig, and R. Wedlich-Soldner. Patchwork organization of the yeast plasma membrane into numerous coexisting domains. *Nat. Cell Biol.*, 14(6):640–648, Jun 2012.

B. L. Sprague and J. G. McNally. Frap analysis of binding: proper and fitting. *Trends in Cell Biology*, 15(2):84–91, 2005.

E. Sprinzak, Y. Altuvia, and H. Margalit. Characterization and prediction of protein-protein interactions within and between complexes. *Proc Natl Acad Sci U S A*, 103(40):14718–23, 2006.

C. Stark, B. J. Breitkreutz, T. Reguly, L. Boucher, A. Breitkreutz, and M. Tyers. Biogrid: a general repository for interaction datasets. *Nucleic Acids Res*, 34(Database issue):D535–9, 2006.

D. Stijn. A cluster algorithm for graphs. Technical report, CWI (Centre for Mathematics and Computer Science), 2000.

A. Strehl and J. Ghosh. Cluster ensembles — a knowledge reuse framework for combining multiple partitions. *J. Mach. Learn. Res.*, 3:583–617, 2003.

V. Strádalová, W. Stahlschmidt, G. Grossmann, M. Blazikova, R. Rachel, W. Tanner, and J. Malínsky. Furrow-like invaginations of the yeast plasma membrane correspond to membrane compartment of can1. *J Cell Sci*, 2009.

S. E. Sund, J. A. Swanson, and D. Axelrod. Cell membrane orientation visualized by polarized total internal reflection fluorescence. *Biophys J*, 77(4):2266–83, 1999.

K. Tarassov, V. Messier, C. R. Landry, S. Radinovic, M. M. Molina, I. Shames, Y. Malitskaya, J. Vogel, and et al. An in vivo map of the yeast protein interactome. *Science*, 2008.

F. J. Theis, N. S. Müller, C. Plant, and C. Böhm. Robust second-order source separation identifies experimental responses in biomedical imaging. In *Proceedings of the 9th international conference on Latent variable analysis and signal separation*, pages 466–73, 1929209, 2010. Springer-Verlag.

J. Tischler, B. Lehner, and A. G. Fraser. Evolutionary plasticity of genetic interaction networks. *Nat Genet*, 40(4):390–1, 2008.

A. H. Tong, G. Lesage, G. D. Bader, H. Ding, H. Xu, X. Xin, J. Young, G. F. Berriz, and et al. Global mapping of the yeast genetic interaction network. *Science*, 303(5659):808–13, 2004.

L. Tong, V. C. Soon, Y. F. Huang, and R. Liu. Amuse: a new blind identification algorithm. In *Circuits and Systems, 1990., IEEE International Symposium on*, pages 1784–7 vol.3, 1990.

M. Uchida, R. R. Mouriño-Pérez, and R. W. Roberson. Total internal reflection fluorescence microscopy of fungi. *Fungal Biology Reviews*, 24(3-4): 132–6, 2011.

N. C. Uwaje, N. S. Mueller, G. Maccarrone, and C. W. Turck. Interrogation of ms/ms search data with an pi filter algorithm to increase protein identification success. *Electrophoresis*, 28(12):1867–74, 2007.

G. Valet, J. F. Leary, and A. Tarnok. Cytomics–new technologies: towards a human cytome project. *Cytometry. Part A : the journal of the International Society for Analytical Cytology*, 59(2):167–71, 2004.

C. Varun, B. Arindam, and K. Vipin. Anomaly detection: A survey. *ACM Computing Surveys*, 2009.

W. F. Velicer. Suppressor variables and the semipartial correlation coefficient. *Educational and Psychological Measurement*, 38(4):953–8, 1978.

N. X. Vinh, J. Epps, and J. Bailey. Information theoretic measures for clusterings comparison: is a correction for chance necessary? In *ICML '09: Proceedings of the 26th Annual International Conference on Machine Learning*, pages 1073–80, 2009.

A. E. Vinogradov. Modularity of cellular networks shows general center-periphery polarization. *Bioinformatics*, 24(24):2814–7, 2008.

W. Voigt, S. Matsui, M. B. Yin, W. C. Burhans, H. Minderman, and Y. M. Rustum. Topoisomerase-i inhibitor sn-38 can induce dna damage and chromosomal aberrations independent from dna synthesis. *Anticancer Research*, 18(5A):3499–505, 1998.

U. von Luxburg. A tutorial on spectral clustering. *Statistics and Computing*, 17(4):395–416, 2007.

Michael Wall, Andreas Rechtsteiner, and Luis Rocha. *Singular Value Decomposition and Principal Component Analysis*, pages 91–109. Kluwel, 2003.

T. C. Walther, J. H. Brickner, P. S. Aguilar, S. Bernales, C. Pantoja, and P. Walter. Eisosomes mark static sites of endocytosis. *Nature*, 439(7079):998–1003, 2006.

J. C. Waters. Accuracy and precision in quantitative fluorescence microscopy. *Journal of Cell Biology*, 185(7):1135–48, 2009.

R. Wedlich-Soldner, S. C. Wai, T. Schmidt, and R. Li. Robust cell polarity is a dynamic state established by coupling transport and gtpase signaling. *The Journal of cell biology*, 166(6):889–900, 2004.

K. Wu, J. H. Dawe, and J. P. Aris. Expression and subcellular localization of a membrane protein related to hsp30p in saccharomyces cerevisiae. *Biochimica et Biophysica Acta*, 1463(2):477–82, 2000.

J. Xie, D. Zhang, and W. Xu. Spatially adaptive wavelet denoising using the minimum description length principle. *IEEE Transactions on Image Processing*, 13(2):179–87, 2004.

T. Yoshida, H. Motoda, and T. Washio. Adaptive ripple down rules method based on minimum description length principle. In *ICDM*, pages 530–7, 2002.

M. E. Young, T. S. Karpova, B. Brügger, D. M. Moschenross, G. K. Wang, R. Schneiter, F. T. Wieland, and J. A. Cooper. The sur7p family defines novel cortical domains in saccharomyces cerevisiae, affects sphingolipid metabolism, and is involved in sporulation. *Mol Cell Biol*, 22(3):927–34, 2002.

L. Zelnik-Manor and P. Perona. Self-tuning spectral clustering. In *Advances in Neural Information Processing Systems*, volume 17, pages 1601–8, 2004.

V. Zinchuk and O. Grossenbacher-Zinchuk. Recent advances in quantitative colocalization analysis: focus on neuroscience. *Prog Histochem Cytochem*, 44(3):125–72, 2009.

B Abbreviations

2D Two-dimensional
AMI Adjusted Mutual Information
BSS Blind Source Separation
CS Control Sample
dGGM differential Gaussian Graphical Model
e.g. example given
EPD Exponential Power Distribution
FastICA Fast implementation of ICA algorithm
FDR False-discovery Rate
FN False Negative
FP False Positive
FRAP Fluorescence Recovery After Photobleaching
FT-ICR Fourier-Transform Ion-Cyclotron-Resonance
GD Gaussian Distribution
GFP Green Fluorescent Protein
GO Gene Onthology
IC Independent Component
ICA Independent Component Analysis
KDD Knowledge Discovery in Databases
LOF Local Outlier Factor
MCL Markov CLuster Algorithm
MDL Minimum Description Length
MS Mass Spectrometry
no. number

PaCCo *Pa*rameter-free *C*lustering by *Co*ding costs
PC   Principle Component
PCA Principal Component Analysis
PDF Probability Density Function
PG   Phosphatidylglycerol
PI   Phosphatidylinositol
pI   isoelectric point
PM   Plasma Membrane
PM   Plasma Membrane
PPI Protein-Protein Interaction
PS   Phosphatidylethanolamine
PS   Phosphatidylserine
PSF Point Spread Function
RFP Red Fluorescent Protein
ROI Region of Interest
SA   Simulated Annealing
SAM Sign Auto-covariance Matrix
SAM-SOBI Sign Autocovariance Matrix - Second Order Blind Identification
SGA Synthetic Genetic Assay
SOBI Second Order Blind Identification
SOI Sample(s) of Interest
TIRF Total Internal Reflection Fluorescence
TP   True Positive
wt   wild type

C Index

Symbols
-ome 2f, 5, 92, 171, 176f
-omics
    cytomics *see* cytome
    interactomics *see* interactome
    lipidomics *see* lipidome
    membrane proteomics *see* membrane proteome
    peptidomics *see* peptidome
    proteomics *see* proteome

A
algorithm
    CoCo *see* CoCo
    dGGM *see* dGGM
    FastICA *see* FastICA
    k-means *see* k-means
    LOCI *see* LOCI
    LOF *see* LOF
    MCL *see* MCL
    Metis *see* Metis
    PaCCo *see* PaCCo
    SAM-SOBI 140
    SOBI *see* SOBI
    X-means *see* X-means

B
BSS 14
    ICA *see* ICA
    PCA *see* PCA

C

Index

CoCo 16ff, 44, 147f, 152–155, 161–170, 175f
coding costs 7, 15, 17f, 31f, 57–60, 62ff, 67, 152ff, 156, 161f, 166, 173
compression 5–8, 15, 17, 206
correlation-based network 9, 23f, 85, 91–95
covariance matrix 23, 92, 94, 156
cytome 2ff, 13ff, 135f, 140, 175

D

data compression 29–33, 45, 56–60, 63, 65, 67, 82, 152ff, 156, 161ff, 166, 170, 172, 176
deconvolution 115f, 120
dGGM 9ff, 85, 98, 102f, 106–110, 174, 176
disease-specific 8–11, 85, 100–104, 106f, 109f

E

eigen decomposition 21, 26, 41, 156
EPD 18, 152ff, 158–163, 168

F

FastICA 39, 142–146, 157
FRAP 14f, 135–146

G

gene ontology 38, 79
GGM 9ff, 24, 85, 95
    dGGM *see* dGGM
Glioblastoma 11, 85, 88, 95ff, 103, 105, 109f, 171, 173f
graph 2, 4–9, 22, 36, 45, 48f, 51–67, 69–74, 77ff, 81f, 172
graph clustering 5ff, 40f, 45–83, 172, 206

I

ICA 14f, 18, 24f, 27f, 38f, 135, 140, 142f, 146, 153f, 156–163, 168, 175f
    FastICA *see* FastICA
    SAM-SOBI *see* SAM-SOBI
    SOBI *see* SOBI
interactome 2–5, 38, 45–50, 53f, 78–83, 172f
interactomics 46

J

jackknife resampling 10, 101

Index

K
k-means 7, 35, 45, 57f, 65, 82
KDD 1, 4, 172, 176f

L
lipidome 2f, 8f, 11, 85ff, 90f, 93, 95ff, 103f, 106, 110, 173f
LOCI 42, 163–166, 168
LOF 43, 163–170

M
mass spectrometry 85, 88
matrix 21
MCL 40, 48, 69ff, 73, 75, 77ff, 81
MDL 7, 17f, 31, 40f, 44f, 56ff, 152f, 161
membrane proteome 2, 11ff, 111f, 116, 123, 125, 134, 176
Metis 40, 69f, 73, 75, 77ff, 81
microscopy images 4, 11–14, 111–146, 174f
modularity 8, 36f, 48, 51, 53, 70, 78f, 81
MS 2, 4, 46, 85f, 88ff, 98f, 104, 108, 148–151

N
network 2–5, 8f, 45–48, 54ff, 70, 79, 82
network factor 119, 123, 125, 131f, 134, 174
network-like 119, 123, 174

O
outlier detection 16, 42f, 147–170, 175

P
PaCCo 6ff, 40f, 45f, 56–63, 65–70, 73, 75, 77–83, 172f, 176f
partial correlation 9, 23, 85, 91–94, 96ff, 100ff, 105, 107
PCA 24ff, 28, 44, 156ff, 160, 163
Pearson correlation 23, 85, 91f, 98, 120f, 126, 131–134
peptidome 2f, 15f, 18, 147–150, 163, 168ff, 175
PPI 3ff, 46ff, 54ff, 78, 82, 134
proteome 2ff, 38, 148, 150

S
SAM-SOBI 14f, 135f, 140, 142–146, 175, 199
simulated annealing 49–54, 79, 82

SOBI 39
spectral clustering 41, 69, 73, 75, 77ff, 81

X
X-Means 44, 163

Y
yeast 5, 12, 14, 47f, 78, 111–134

D Glossary

-ome is the suffix typically used for each type of object analyzed in the respective field. When referring to the studies conducted to analyze an -ome the suffix **-omics** is used. 2, 3, 5, 92, 171, 176, 177

CoCo is a outlier detection algorithm developed as part of my doctoral work. *CoCo* coupled a flexible definition of regular data to data compression. The idea was to define a reliable measure of outlierness. 16–18, 44, 147, 148, 152–155, 161–170, 175, 176

coding costs are the costs required to transfer information through a communication channel from sender to receiver. The terms compression costs, transfer costs or communication costs may all be interchangeably used to describe the same principle: The compression costs of dataset give an estimate how expensive the communication costs between sender and receiver are, whereby the costs required to physically transfer the dataset are the transfer cost. 7, 15, 17, 18, 31, 32, 57–60, 62–64, 67, 152–154, 156, 161, 162, 166, 173

cytome are behaviors on and of single cells. For example, those proteins currently expressed in one cell are analyzes with respect to its dynamic behavior over time contributing to the cell's phenotype. When referring to the studies on a organism's cytome, the term **cytomics** is used. 2–4, 13–15, 135, 136, 140, 175

deconvolution is an image restoration technique and basically reverts the physical imaging process in which fluorescent objects are characteristically blurred – thus convolved. Since convolution is technically never noise-free the algorithm to deconvolve an image has to account for image noise. A deconvolved image is the result of an image restoration algorithm performing a deconvolution. 115, 116, 120

dGGM is a novel principle to unravel only the disease-specific correlations and was developed as part of my doctoral work. Studies usually conduct experiments with many control samples and only one or few sample(s) of interest (SOI). Especially false positive correlations may occur when correlations were calculated from the entire dataset whereof solely few data points were actually biologically relevant. The dGGM method was solving this problem. 9–11, 85, 98, 102, 103, 106–110, 174, 176

disease-specific are those correlations in my doctoral work, which are most relevant to the disease (**disease-relevant**). To determine which correlation is indeed disease-specific, the sample of interest – the sample related to the target phenotype analyzed – is exploited for analysis. 8–11, 85, 100–104, 106, 107, 109, 110

Glioblastoma are human brain tumors and their *in vitro* model is the U87 cell line. The U87 GM cell lines carry the wt p53 tumor sup- pressor gene, and not a mutant version. 11, 85, 88, 95–97, 103, 105, 109, 110, 171, 173, 174

interactome describes the interacting profile of a molecule type. For example, proteins interact to perform cellular functions. The PPI networks are graphs holding the physical or genetic interaction information of protein or protein encoding genes, respectively. The assembly of all those (physical) protein interactions is a protein-protein interaction (PPI) network. Interactions may also occur on genetical level yielding genetic interaction networks. The studies of cell's interactome are termed **interactomics**. In my doctoral work, the interactome mainly relates to the genetic interaction networks. 2–5, 38, 46, 48, 50, 53, 78–80, 172, 173

KDD is the term used to define the process retrieving knowledge from a raw dataset. After data selection and data processing, data may be transformed prior to be mined by data mining techniques. Finally, data evaluation is also part of the KDD knowledge retrieval process. 1, 4, 172, 176, 177

lipidome is the set of lipids currently present in a cell. When referring to the studies on a organism's lipidome, the term **lipidomics** is used. Lipids are mainly found in cellular membranes which encompass and compartmentalize each living cell. 2, 3, 8, 9, 11, 85–87, 90, 91, 93, 95–97, 103, 104, 106, 110, 173, 174

MDL is the minimum description length which is used to numerically evaluate the coding costs.. 7, 17, 18, 31, 40, 41, 44, 45, 56–58

membrane proteome is the collection of all membrane proteins of a cell. In our studies we only refer to those proteins associated with the plasma membrane of the cell. As part of membranes, the membrane proteome is building an active interface between the cell and its environment. We termed the studies on the membrane proteome **membrane proteomics**. Subsequently, the membrane proteome is a true subset of the proteome. 2, 11–13, 111, 112, 116, 123, 125, 134, 176

network is typically used interchangeably with the term graph. A graph is the data type to represent a network interlinking nodes in an undirected or directed manner. Networks refer to a part of all graph types, but e.g. district from rooted graphs, the trees. 1, 3–5, 8, 9, 45–48, 54–56, 70, 79, 82. **Network factor** is a factor derived during my work to quantification of spatial patterns of images. We observed distinct but closely related patterns from patch- to network-like structures eventually quantified with the network factor. 119, 123, 125, 131, 132, 134, 174. **Network-like** is a termed used to describe a spatial pattern of PM proteins. 119, 123, 174.

PaCCo is a weighted graph clustering algorithm developed as part of my doctoral work. Data compression was exploited for weighted graph clustering. *PaCCo* fully automatic algorithm, which was not only noise robust but also clustered parameter-independently. 6–8, 40, 41, 45, 46, 56–63, 65–70, 73, 75, 77–83, 172, 173, 176, 177

peptidome is the collection of peptides in a cell. Proteins are long chains of amino acids, while peptides are short amino acid polymers. Digestion of proteins results in the set of peptides. Studies of the peptidome are termed **peptidomics**. 2, 3, 15, 16, 18, 147–150, 163, 168–170, 175

proteome A proteome consists of all proteins that are expressed in a cell at a given time and situation. Thus, it is a subset of all possible gene products encoded in the genome. 2–4, 38, 148, 150

i want morebooks!

Buy your books fast and straightforward online - at one of world's fastest growing online book stores! Environmentally sound due to Print-on-Demand technologies.

Buy your books online at
www.get-morebooks.com

Kaufen Sie Ihre Bücher schnell und unkompliziert online – auf einer der am schnellsten wachsenden Buchhandelsplattformen weltweit! Dank Print-On-Demand umwelt- und ressourcenschonend produziert.

Bücher schneller online kaufen
www.morebooks.de

VDM Verlagsservicegesellschaft mbH
Heinrich-Böcking-Str. 6-8   Telefon: +49 681 3720 174   info@vdm-vsg.de
D - 66121 Saarbrücken   Telefax: +49 681 3720 1749 www.vdm-vsg.de

Printed by Books on Demand GmbH, Norderstedt / Germany